ANIMAL HEROES

ANIMAL HEROES

Stories of Courageous Family Pets and
Animals in the Wild

Byron G. Wels

Macmillan Publishing Co., Inc.
New York
Collier Macmillan Publishers
London

Macmillan Publishing Co., Inc.
866 Third Avenue, New York, N.Y. 10022
Collier Macmillan Canada, Ltd.

The photograph of Turkey is courtesy of the ASPCA.
All other photographs are courtesy of Ken-L-Ration.

Library of Congress Cataloging in Publication Data

Wels, Byron G
    Animal heroes

    1. Pets—Legends and stories. 2. Animals,
Legends and stories. 3. Working animals—Legends
and stories. I. Title.
SF416.W47   818'.5'407   79-16989
ISBN 0-02-625910-9

First Printing 1979

Printed in the United States of America

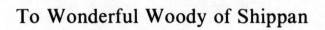

To Wonderful Woody of Shippan

CONTENTS

FOREWORD

An old army sergeant once said to me, "Son, if a woman is interested, you don't have to do a thing. And if she's not interested, there's nothing at all that you can do."

Does that seem like a strange way to begin a book about animal heroes? Perhaps. But in attempting to explain the love that a man can have for an animal, and the love that an animal can have for a man, the effort required depends solely on whom you're trying to explain it all to. If you're trying to tell an animal lover about it, you needn't bother at all. He already understands. And if you're going to try to explain it to somebody who has never been owned by a dog, don't waste your breath. He'll tell you that such love is simply the animal's way of securing itself, that an animal that lays down its life for a human is merely the victim of circumstance.

We who know and love animals know better. Animals do indeed love the people they live with. While some are more demonstrative than others, people, too, are different in the ways they show affection for one another.

There's a word that begins to loom in importance here. That word is *anthropomorphism*. It is a process through which humans imbue their animals with human qualities. The doting dowager who holds her little Yorkshire terrier cradled in her arms may say, "He says 'thank you,'" when her pet is offered a treat by a friend. Of course animals are not human, and while they may not think as humans do, those of us who know them well can come to recognize subtle alterations of expression on the seemingly stolid faces of our pets. We've seen our dogs smile, even laugh! We know when they're sorry about something, when they're contrite, and yes, even when they're angry. Who can doubt the total puzzlement that is expressed when the head is cocked to one side, one ear raised almost questioningly? If your dog were suddenly blessed with speech, he couldn't say more clearly, "I don't understand."

What is this book all about? The title, *Animal Heroes*, doesn't begin to tell the whole story. Basically, it's a book about many animals who have selflessly offered their own lives to save the lives of humans. But it's so very much more than that.

This book is about love.

Animals respond to love by offering love in return. If you treat your animals with love, with respect, show affection to them and do so often, they will respond in kind. When you come home after being away all day, does your pet listlessly open one eye as though to say, "Oh, you're home, are you?" Or does he suddenly come to life— gamboling at your feet, leaping about you in great joy—so that you know he's happy to see you again?

Love for an animal is an investment that pays great dividends. Show the meager kindness of a pat on his head, and he'll repay you by licking your face.

Frankly, that's what animals are all about. Being devoid of speech, they can only listen when you speak. But they are supersensitive to emotion and respond to love in an open, uninhibited fashion that few humans can match without embarrassment. The man who might be embarrassed to publicly demonstrate affection to his own family will unhesitatingly show open affection to his dog. Loving an animal is a good and healthy thing, and not something to be ashamed of.

In this book, we're going to be talking about many animals. Not just dogs and cats, although they will certainly receive their fair share, but about all sorts of animals. And try to remember that while your own family pet may not be mentioned in this book, the love that is shared between you makes that pet as important in your life as any animal that is described here. Surely, given the need and the opportunity, there is no feat of valor described in this book that your own pet would not gladly emulate.

I suppose that, in the final analysis, that's what this book is all about. It's love of a very special and important kind. And, too, the book is written for those who know and love animals and who know the love of an animal for them. The others? Those who don't know? They never will understand, will they?

But we—you and I and our pets—we *do* know and we *do* understand.

Sarge was right.

Byron G. Wels

ANIMAL HEROES

CHAPTER ONE

THE LEGEND

Animals have shared the earth with mankind for as long as mankind has been here. It is only natural, therefore, that many of the old stories and legends that sprang up about man should also involve animals. Unfortunately, most of these legends are difficult to document, for they have been transmitted by word of mouth, handed down from generation to generation, probably becoming somewhat distorted in the process.

Remus and Romulus, the founders of the city of Rome, were said to have been raised by wolves in the wild. Statues have been erected depicting the two children suckling at the breasts of a wolf.

Legend recounts the tale of Androcles, who happened on a lion in the wilderness, a lion who was howling and suffering intense pain from a thorn in its foot. Androcles overcame his fear and extracted the thorn, relieving the lion's pain. Later, Androcles was captured by the Romans and forced to fight a lion in the arena. It happened that this was the same lion he had befriended. The lion remembered Androcles and, instead of devouring him, submitted to friendship and petting.

1

Noah, too, was a friend to animals. His ark is credited with saving two members of each species that walked the face of the earth. If you are inclined to think of this as a mere fable, consider the fact that the reputed remnants of Noah's ark have recently been discovered, and at exactly the place that the Bible story documents.

Man's friendship with animals has been immortalized in song and story, including the little song about Ferdinand the bull who'd rather sit under a tree and smell the flowers than fight the toreadors.

Man has always divided animals into two categories— those that are friend and those that are foe. In early American history, the pioneers made that distinction and it still applies today. There are "varmints" and "critters." Varmints are those animal pests that are never domesticated and that prey on man and his belongings. To this day a bounty or reward is given for the pelts of some of these varmints. The only way that man can seem to get along with them is by destroying them. Critters (creatures) are another matter. They can be domesticated or, if wild, can still manage to share the earth with mankind, living in peaceful harmony.

A further distinction is drawn worldwide between those animals that are domestic and those that are wild. The domestic animals share more than living space with man, for they also help to shoulder his burdens. Draft animals, for example, provide man with meat, milk, skins, and other products that are the very necessities of life. Wild animals, on the other hand, not only refuse to domicile with man, but may even be predatory and attack man and his belongings.

Man has only recently recognized the rights of wild animals and has declared some of them to be endangered species, thus assuring them protection against the violence and destruction that might otherwise be their lot.

Animals and man often ally with each other for their common good, forming a bond that is almost symbiotic. As an example, consider the teamwork of hunting. Man cannot seek out and find the game that will feed him, at least not as well as a hunting dog. On the other hand, the dog is unable to fire a gun to bring that game down. The dog finds the game, signals where it is, man fires the gun, and then both dog and man are able to eat!

The horse has not the skill or knowledge to plant, and man hasn't the strength to plow. Together, they can raise the grain that will feed both.

In the underdeveloped countries, a beast of burden can be rented, along with its master, to perform heavy tasks. When the work is completed, the man's wages include enough to feed himself, his family and the beast as well.

How did it all begin? The relationship between man and animals goes back to prehistoric times, before man began to record his own history for the benefit of posterity. The growth of the relationship depended on the state of man's evolutionary development as well as the state of development of the beast. And, of course, the history of man and beast working together is different for each type of beast you're talking about!

One of the most common animal-man relationships is that of man and dog. This pairing is typical of the way such relationships began and grew.

In early days, animals such as jackals used to follow man and scavenge his leavings. It was far easier for these doglike creatures to take the leftovers of man's predations than to do their own hunting.

Man eventually learned that the jackal, a natural hunter, was more adept at locating game. It took to moving out in packs to nip, bark at, and otherwise harass the prey, often working to drive the game toward bands of men who were waiting with their spears.

Occasionally, one of the doglike animals would be killed in the pursuit. When a mother of young cubs was killed, and the cubs were taken by man into his home, the process of domestication began. And when the cubs grew to adulthood and mated with other animals of the same species, they produced the first cubs born in domesticity. The process of domestication was in full swing.

3

Before long, man learned that certain traits and attributes were prevalent in some breeds, missing in others. Controlled breeding was initiated, giving rise to the various breeds, each of which had its own specific function in life. Greyhounds were bred for speed. Massive-bodied work dogs were best suited to heavy chores. Other dogs with sharp sense of smell were used for hunting and scenting.

During the days of the early English courts, dogs with long, shaggy coats were given free run of the dining halls. Eating utensils and napkins were not used, and when one of the diners got his hands greasy on a piece of fowl or a joint of mutton, he simply wiped his hands on the dog's fur!

Horses have also been bred for specific tasks. The draft animal is far different physically from the racer. And these categories have been further broken down. As every racing aficionado can tell you, there are two types of sulky racers—the pacer and the trotter.

All horses, however, go back to a prehistoric animal called *Eohippus*. This common ancestor looked vaguely the way a horse does today, except that it had a larger head in proportion to the body, had a three-toed foot (which has since evolved into a two-toed foot or hoof, with the third toe forming the fetlock), and was about as large as today's medium-sized dog. Compare this with the massive Percheron draft horses that are used to pull beer wagons in Europe, and you can see that only the vaguest relationship exists.

Getting back to dogs, one of the most famous breeds is the St. Bernard, used for rescue work in the Alps. Most people are under the impression that this massive dog runs to a downed mountaineer with a cask of brandy about its neck—and stands there patiently while the poor snowbound person helps himself to a swig of alcohol. It's hard to figure out exactly what happens next in the minds of the people who believe this myth. Does the fallen person simply take a big swig of brandy and then get up as good as new and follow the dog back to the hospice where he and the monks have

4

some more brandy and sing old songs for the rest of the night?

Actually, the truth is quite different. These dogs have an instinct about snow. They can tell when an avalanche is coming and have actually been known to get up and move aside just before a pile of snow lands right where they had been sitting or lying! St. Bernards are trained to go out in groups. They locate a person who has fallen in the snow, uncover him if he is buried, and then lie next to or atop him to provide warmth while one of the team returns to get human assistance. The dogs who wait will keep the person warm and, should he be unconscious, will lick his face until consciousness returns.

Dogs have always been kept as pets. Alexander Pope, the poet, recalled that on the collar of the dog owned by the then Prince of Wales was the little poem—could we call it "doggerel"?—that read:

> I am his highness' dog at Kew
> Pray tell me, sir, whose dog are you?

One of the saddest tales in all of the animal world recounts an injustice that was performed by the Welsh prince Llewellyn in the thirteenth century. It seems that Llewellyn saw his dog, a Wolfhound, coming out of his house covered with blood. Llewellyn rushed into the house and saw his son's cradle overturned and lying in a pool of drying blood. Jumping to the conclusion that the dog had killed the baby, Llewellyn drew his sword and killed the dog.

Then he turned back to the house and learned what had really happened. A wolf had entered the house and the dog had killed the wolf to save the baby, which was now crying under the cradle. The body of the dead wolf gave mute testimony to what had happened. The dog's name was Gelert, and to this day there is a village in North Wales called Beddgelert, of "Gelert's grave." A stone marks the supposed burial place.

There is, despite the touching beauty of this legend, some question as to its authenticity. Folk historians say that the tale was invented by a ballad singer of the eighteenth century and that the town was really named for Saint Kelert.

The love affair between man and dog often reaches beyond the grave. Dogs are relatively short-lived in comparison to man, and some dogs have so touched their masters that they have been entombed in special pet cemeteries, along with touching and beautiful tombstone inscriptions.

> Only a dog, but such love he gave
> Cannot have perished in the grave.
> So constant and faithful and true a heart
> Must in eternity have some part.
> And sometimes I fancy
> When I've crossed life's sea
> I'll find him waiting to welcome me.

A most touching editorial in the *Portland Oregonian* reads as follows:

Where to Bury a Dog

There is only one best place to bury a dog. If you bury him in this spot, he will come to you when you call—come to you over the dim, grim frontiers of death, and down the well-remembered path, and to your side again. And though you call a dozen living dogs to heel they shall not growl at him, nor resent his coming, for he belongs there. People may scoff at you, who see no lightest blade of grass bent by his footfall, who hear no whimper, people who may never really have had a dog. Smile at them, for you shall know something that is hidden from them, and which is well worth the knowing. The one best place to bury a good dog is in the heart of his master.

As you can see, the love relationship between man and beast is a very close one, and while man has the ability to write, carve, and otherwise bestow his thoughts on a lost friend, it's nevertheless a two-way street. Perhaps the animal hasn't the skills to leave his love for his master for an eternity—a written poem of love for future generations to wonder at—but don't get the idea that the love is not returned.

Every year, a serious and solemn ceremony takes place at the Shibuya railroad station in Tokyo, Japan. Hundreds of dog lovers appear and pay homage to the memory of Hachiko, an Akita dog belonging to Dr. Eisaburo Ueno, who taught at Tokyo University.

Every morning, the faithful dog would walk with his master to the railroad station, and Dr. Ueno would get on the train for the university. Each afternoon, the Akita would come to the station just before the train came in. He would wait, greet his master, and walk home with him. Then one May evening in 1925 Dr. Ueno did not step off the train to greet his dog. He had suffered a heart attack at the university and died. The dog waited until midnight for his master's return, and every evening, until his death nine years later, the dog came to the station and awaited the doctor's return. There was no way to stop the dog or dissuade him from his vigil. It was not until the dog's own death in March 1934 that his presence was missed at the station.

The fidelity of Hachiko was known throughout Japan, and on his death, newspaper stories carred the tale all over the world. Contributions poured in, and a statue was erected to the memory of this loyal animal, who throughout his life kept the memory of his dead master in his heart.

The Newfoundland has also carved his place in history as an animal hero. This excellent water dog—also called a "Newf" or a "Newfie"—is a large, massive working breed, bred to help fishermen handle heavy nets. Newfoundlands have saved many drowning persons, thanks to their skills in the water and their great strength and bulk.

One famous story concerns a Newf who was called upon to rescue the crew of a foundering ship that had run aground in high seas. The ship was fast breaking apart. A group of men on shore looked on helplessly, for the turbulent waters made rescue totally impossible. The people on the ship were doomed to a watery death, and there was nothing that could be done about it except to watch them die and offer up a prayer.

One of the men on shore happened to have his big Newfoundland with him. Thinking quickly, he attached a long line to the dog's collar. "Go get 'em!" he ordered, and the dog leaped selflessly into the roiling waters. He swam strongly toward the doomed ship, battling his way through the rough waters, his progress slow, but progress nonetheless. Finally, he reached the distressed hulk, and the men on the deck pulled him to safety. There, they grabbed the line around his neck and pulled in a stronger, heavier line which had been attached to it by the men on shore. This was made fast to a high point on the ship, and a breeches buoy was towed to the ship from the shore. One by one, the crew were pulled to safety by the men on the shore.

Finally, when only the dog and one man were left on the boat, the people on shore again sent the breeches buoy to the ship, fully expecting that the last man would now be drawn to safety. However, when the buoy was pulled in, it was not the man but the Newfoundland that they had hauled to the safety of the shore. One more trip for the buoy, and the last man was saved, perilous instants before the ship finally broke apart and went to a watery grave!

Foolhardy for the man to have risked his life to save the dog? Not really, when you consider that the dog had saved numbers of lives at great risk to his own. The people on the shore could not have effected this rescue. Only the dog—the Newfoundland—was able to do it. And he didn't balk or hesitate for a moment, but plunged into the waters without a thought for himself.

Again, a fitting tribute to a Newfoundland is carved as an epitaph, as follows:

Beneath this spot
are deposited the remains of a being
who was possessed of beauty without vanity,
strength without insolence,
courage without ferocity,
and all the virtues of man without his vices.
This praise would be empty flattery
were it inscribed upon the ashes of a human being.
And yet it is only what is due to the memory
of the dog BOATSWAIN
Born in Newfoundland, May, 1801
Died at Windsor, 18th November, 1815.

Animals have also shared the burden of men's wars. Their devotion and dedication often exceeds that of their masters. A German shepherd, simply because he is a "German" shepherd, has never been known to refuse assistance to a soldier of another country.

The following is an excerpt from an article written by Lt. Col. E. H. Richardson, Commandant of the British War-Dog School, about the services of the Irish Terriers:

I can say with decided emphasis that the Irish Terriers of the service more than did their part. Many a soldier is alive today through the effort of one of these very terriers. Isolated with his unit in some advanced position, entirely cut off from the main body by a wall of shells, and thus prevented communicating his position or circumstance by telephone or runner so that help might follow, this messenger dog was often the only means his officers had of carrying the dispatch which eventually would bring relief. My opinion of this breed is indeed a high one. They are highly sensitive, spirited dogs of fine mettle, and those of us who respect and admire the fine qualities of mind will find them amply reflected in these terriers. They are extraordinarily intelligent, faithful, and honest, and a man who has one of them as a companion will never lack a true friend.

9

Naturally, any animal living in such close propinquity to man is going to be the subject of some foolish rumors. There are, believe it or not, thousands, nay, hundreds of thousands, of people who *know*—know beyond a doubt—that the only way to train a puppy is to rub his nose in his own dirt if he has an accident in the house and to beat him with a rolled-up newspaper or magazine if he fails to obey a command the first time it is given. Nothing could be further from the truth. I am often tempted to subject people who make such claims to the selfsame torture to see how they like it!

A neighbor who recently acquired a puppy asked if he could have a couple of shotgun shells. For what? He had heard that if you mix gunpowder with a puppy's food, he'll grow up "mean."

Needless to say, he did not get the shells. Gunpowder will not affect a dog in any way—except perhaps to make him sick! The really puzzling question was why he or anyone else would want a mean dog.

Some people get a cruel sort of gratification from having a dog obey their orders and commands. This is entirely the wrong reason to own a dog, but individuals with such ideas regularly appear at obedience schools asking to have their dogs trained for guard and attack. Usually the dogs brought in with this request are broken in spirit, already thoroughly cowed by cruel masters with the wrong purpose in mind.

You should know that unhappy dogs will often try to run away. Animals are highly sensitive and will not willingly stay where they are unwanted and mistreated.

Most dogs who live in a family situation will attach themselves to one member of the family. When the dog is a puppy and in need of kindness, love, and attention, chances are he may spend much of his time with the lady of the house, accepting her as a surrogate mother. In time, as the dog matures, he often transfers his loyalty and affection to the man of the house accepting him as the "leader." I do not mean to imply that other family members are ignored. They are simply accepted for what they are—other family members.

The dog's breed will also give you some information as to its characteristics. People who own shepherds, for example, know that the dog is not happy unless the family—his "flock"—is all nicely collected in one place. At night, he'll make the rounds to see that everybody is properly in bed, and then fall asleep himself, usually at some central point where he can keep an eye on things.

Very often, dogs can be spoiled to the point where they become completely insufferable. Allow the dog to sleep on your bed and you'll have your hands full when you try to break him of the habit. Feed him table scraps and you might just as well set a place for him at the dinner table. Doting dowagers have been known to do just that!

Another common misconception is that all dogs hate all cats. It just isn't so. Get a young dog, then bring a young cat into the house, and while there may be some animosity at the beginning—for the dog will resent any intruder in his own domain—the chances are that an armed neutrality will soon evolve. This will develop into tolerance, and before long you'll find that your dog has adopted the cat as a pet of his own!

Given the right sort of personality, the right set of circumstances, and a family situation in which the male figure is not obviously dominant, the dog himself may elect to step in and fill that role, becoming demanding and overbearing, and actually cowing the other family members.

Some breeds suffer horribly at the hands of know-it-all rumor mongers. Certain breeds have been branded as "vicious," and all dogs of that breed are tarred with the same brush. The ignorant may say things like "That dog will 'turn.'" This is apparently supposed to mean that the dog will revert to its wild state and "turn" upon his master. Somehow, the ignoramuses who are fond of such statements always seem to have an endless supply of "typical" examples to "prove" that dogs have done just that.

A certain pompous, overbearing lady once attended an

obedience trial, just to see how it was done. A few weeks later, her friend purchased a small dog for her child, and the lady, Mrs. Pomposity, declared that she was an "expert" in dog training and would come over to "examine" the dog.

With everybody watching, she took the dog's leash, stood on the wrong side, and said, "Heel!" The dog simply sat there. "Down!" she commanded. The puppy looked at her quizzically.

"I'm sorry," she said, "but this dog is not trainable. Take him back. Get your money back."

Well, the youngster, who by now had fallen in love with the dog, burst into tears. The pompous woman strode out of the house, for she felt she had done her level best. She recounted the story later, and I explained to her that dogs may go to obedience school for months—for years—to learn these things. A little puppy could hardly be expected to obey those commands at the first sitting.

"Well, in my opinion," she countered....

"Your opinion is worthless" was the only comment I could make.

All dogs of a given breed are not alike. They are not all either intelligent or stupid. It's all a matter of training and patience.

At one time, I owned a German shepherd bitch named "Schatzi." She was thoroughly obedience-trained and had taken so many obedience courses that when the graduation certificates were being filled out, I was asked, "What would you like on her certificate? 'Intermediate?'" "No," I offered, "she's already got that one." "How about 'Advanced?'" "No, she's got one of those too." I broke into laughter during the presentation of the certificates, for there, above the word "course," was noted the fact that Schatzi had passed the "Secretarial" course!

Schatzi had been taught to obey hand signals and had learned to watch for them. She didn't have to hear an uttered word to know we wanted her to "sit," "stay," or "come." One Sunday morning, my wife was in bed watching television with the kids. Schatzi was lying alongside my wife, fast asleep. I looked the situation over and said, "Schatzi, move." She balefully opened one eye and looked at me to see if I meant business. "Move!" I said. She didn't. Now the kids got into the act. "She was there first, Dad!" "Yeah," I replied, "but it's *my* bed."

I looked at her again and tried to reason. "Schatzi, I want to lie down."

What happened next evoked gales of laughter, for Schatzi raised one paw, then lowered it to the bed. She had given the hand signal for "down"!

Dogs have to participate as family members, and Schatzi was no exception. One day, the kids were playing "Ring Around the Rosie" in our living room, and Schatzi wanted to get into the game. They opened the ring, and two of them took hold of her collar. They sang the little song, moved in a circle, and at the command "All fall *down!*" Schatzi went down, too. She knew what that meant!

The next night at obedience school, I got a few volunteers for a quick game of "Ring Around the Rosie" and demonstrated Schatzi's skill. Later, during class, the instructor said, "Down your dogs!" and somebody started singing "Ring Around the Rosie!"

Animals in the wild state sometimes form alliances with mankind on those occasions that require this for their own good. But these relationships quickly dissolve when the need for them is over. Many people have befriended wild animals and have even attempted to rear wild animal babies which appear to be docile and tractable. However, when the animals achieve adulthood, the instinct to return to the wild may reassert itself and the animals may become dangerous. Unfortunately, it is usually unfair to simply dump such an animal back in the wild, for it may be unable to care for itself. The hunting instinct is a "learned" instinct, and a wild animal that has been raised in domesticity often has no idea how to hunt and kill for itself.

People identify with animals, and in our own modern mythology, as represented by movies and television, animals

13

are depicted as heroes all the time. Who can forget the adventures of Lassie, the collie, in *Lassie, Come Home*? Or if you hark back even earlier, surely you recall the *Adventures of Rin-Tin-Tin.*

The height of anthropomorphism occurs in television cartoons. Such characters as Deputy Dawg, Alvin and the Chipmunks, and a wide assortment of other animals, both wild and domestic, perform heroically every Saturday morning.

Other heroic animals on television have included Roy Rogers's horse Trigger, and in the old movies, don't forget veteran cowboy actor Tom Mix and his horse Tony. It wasn't all horses and dogs either, for surely you recall Flipper, that denizen of the deep. And if you care to stretch a point, our own mythology has to include the famous talking horse Mr. Ed.

What's the source of animal heroism? Well, you must remember that in his relationship with domestic animals, man has always had the upper hand. The animal relinquishes control to man and accepts food, shelter, and love in return. Wild animals, in contrast, are unwilling to sacrifice their freedom to man, regardless of what may be offered in exchange.

The domestic animal computes the exchange as a fair one. He usually leads a comfortable, easy-going life and does not have to hunt for his own food. The animal's decision to accept this arrangement is not made on a conscious level, of course. It's just something that happens, and both man and beast accept it as such.

But love is a strange thing, and the love that an animal can have for a human is often overpowering. The preservation of life is as important to an animal as it is to a human.

Let's look at heroics for a moment. Heroism cannot be planned. Faced with inordinate risk—risk that endangers life and limb—it takes a special something to put your life on the line for another. Yet men who have performed heroically in battle, when interviewed later, were at a loss to explain their actions. They didn't plan to be heroic, but faced with a lethal situation they unhesitantly rushed in and took the risk, emerging as heroes afterward.

It's really not much different with animals. An animal, faced with a situation that threatens the people he loves, can behave in a heroic fashion, regardless of the danger. What makes the animal do this? Love and nothing else. The love he bears for the people he saves is so overpowering that it supersedes any danger he may face.

Remember, too, that animals do not reason the way humans do. Humans will consider the odds, weigh the probabilities, and then make a rational decision on the basis of the information available to them. Animals operate on the level of instinct and are motivated to perform by love.

The very same forces, in the final analysis, motivate man and beast to heroic proportion. Heroism is not something unique to a specific sort of personality. Given the right kind of motivation and a special sort of situation, heroism can occur in either man or beast.

It should also be borne in mind that heroism need not always be on a grand scale. Naturally, the rewards will always go to the big and dramatic rescues, but an act of heroism on the part of an animal need not necessarily be big and dramatic.

The little Yorkshire terrier that bravely barks at a sound at the door is—in his own way, and in proportion to his size—as heroic as the larger dog that actually attacks an intruder.

Animals are aware of their ability to be heroic. Many dogs who are just "family pets" will bark at a real or imagined sound merely to call attention to themselves, and, having thus challenged this unseen (and possibly nonexistent) enemy, they will come to you for a pat on the head as a reward for guarding the premises so devotedly.

CHAPTER TWO

ANIMAL
WAR HEROES

In time of war, animals have always played a significant role. The U.S. Army has a special section, the K-9 Corps, devoted to the training and handling of animals for military action. The K-9 Corps's existence testifies not only to the confidence placed in animals by the army but also to the esteem in which they are held by their human comrades.

In the heat of battle, when death-laden bullets are flying, it is safer for soldiers to remain in trenches and foxholes than to expose themselves needlessly on the battlefield. However, it is often necessary that information or material be conveyed under fire from place to place. Animals, considered more expendable than men, are used for such communication.

Dogs are also used for guard patrol duties, either on their own or in the company of a man. Should an enemy penetrate the perimeter of a secured area, he will find himself faced with a vicious guard dog that bares his teeth and snarls a challenge. The animal's threat is very real, for the chances are great that the enemy may suffer severe bodily damage.

The K-9 Corps animal is merely doing the job for which he was trained. Is this, then, heroic action? Of course not. If

17

it were, we could easily fill the pages of this volume and several others like it.

But occasionally, a special case emerges, one in which the actions of an expendable animal stand out far above the norm. It is this outstanding action that is praiseworthy, that is noted, often unrewarded, but still of such dimension that it begs attention. It is this sort of heroism that we spell forth in these pages.

During World War II, the 899th Field Artillery had a mascot. In the due course of time, she whelped a litter of six pups, mostly German shepherd. Of the six, the only one to live was a tough little fellow named Blackfoot. When his mother died, Blackfoot was made the organization's mascot.

He soon became "Private Blackfoot," and he spent some time in Louisiana, training with the 899th until they were ready for combat and were shipped overseas. As you can imagine, getting the mascot on board ship was a difficult feat, overseen by S.Sgt. Paul Carden and Pvt. Fred Downs, the dog's guardians. Private Blackfoot was an opinionated sort, and keeping him quiet was not an easy task. But it was especially necessary during the in-port inspection, for had Blackfoot sounded off, he would surely have been found out and left at home.

A dose of morphine did the job, and Blackfoot slept quietly for two and one half days. When the outfit landed in France, the dog was a bit woozy at first, but quickly recovered his senses and was soon ready for battle.

Like most GIs, Blackfoot soon learned how to handle himself under field conditions. Sure, he was there to fight a war, but at the same time, there was no need to be foolishly dedicated, right? He learned how to "buck a chow line" and be the first to get to where the food was. He learned how and when to hit a foxhole so that his life would not be endangered.

During the Battle of the Bulge, Blackfoot sniffed out a German machine gun nest and led his companions to it. A couple of well-placed hand grenades shut the nest and earned Blackfoot his first award, an unofficial Bronze Star.

Blackfoot did a great deal more than that. His soldier friends claim that he "fought" his way across two continents, besting not only enemy opponents but canine ones as well—some two hundred of them in America, England, France, the Netherlands, and Germany!

A mascot is supposed to bring good fortune, and Blackfoot was no slouch there either. In spite of all the action that the 899th saw, not a single man was killed, and only six were wounded. After the war, Blackfoot returned to Camp Shanks with his men, proudly wearing three battle stars, indicating that, like them, he had fought through three campaigns.

Many of the heroic war dogs mentioned in dispatches were recruited informally as pets or mascots of the troops they served with. Others, recruited as service dogs, were often volunteered by their civilian families to a program in World War II called "Dogs for Defense." Chips, one such dog, was a husky–collie–shepherd mix. He was enlisted by his owners, the Edward J. Wrens, of Pleasantville, New York.

Chips received both the Purple Heart and the Distinguished Service Cross for gallantry in action.

When American troops landed on the island of Sicily, Chips, along with his handler, Pvt. John R. Rowell, was a part of the landing force. Enemy machine gunners, working out of a machine gun pillbox disguised as a peasant hut, were decimating the American troops. The American forces were pinned down on the beach. Private Rowell released Chips, who immediately and selflessly sprang to the attack.

Chips made his way to the enemy bunker and leaped at the throat of one of the Italian machine gunners, causing the man to emerge from the pillbox, happy simply to be free of the menacing animal. Chips returned and drove the other two gunners from hiding, securing the pillbox single-handedly.

In addition to the Distinguished Service Cross, this

gallant dog also received the Silver Star for bravery in the face of the enemy.

Chips was three years old at the time, and had as a result of his distinguished military career met such notables as President Franklin Delano Roosevelt, Sir Winston Churchill, and General Dwight D. Eisenhower.

Caesar was a four-year-old German shepherd assigned to duty as a messenger with the marines on Bougainville during World War II. For two days and two nights, Caesar took care of the delivery of all messages between the forward lines and the base camp under withering enemy fire. On the third night, Caesar and his handler, Pvt. Rufus Mayo of Birmingham, Alabama, were halted by a road block some five hundred yards from the American lines. They made for the nearest foxhole to seek refuge.

Caesar detected the unmistakable odor of the enemy and snarled quietly to himself. Soon, one of the enemy appeared, preparing to throw a hand grenade into the foxhole—a hand grenade that, if it went off, would surely spell the end of Private Mayo and Caesar. But Caesar leaped from the foxhole, clamping his viselike jaws around the enemy's wrist. Caesar hadn't waited for an order but had taken action entirely on his own. The enemy screamed and retreated, with Caesar hot on his heels.

Shortly, Mayo heard two shots in rapid succession and before long saw Caesar limping back toward the foxhole. The dog had taken two rifle shots, one in his side and one in his rump. Caesar was later evacuated by stretcher and brought to the base hospital, just as any human hero would have been. Happily, he recovered and lived a full and contented life.

On the other side of the ledger was Boots, who was not actually a war dog. He wandered into the tent area at the 12th Combat Cargo Squadron stationed at the North Field in Myitkyina (Mich-in-naw), Burma, during World War II. Boots was more of a pet than anything else, but being around the squadron's fliers, it wasn't long before he got taken along on a couple of missions. Soon he was seen sporting a jacket made of the remnants of a flight jacket, decorated with the familiar Chinese flag and blood chit. The jacket also had a set of aircrew wings that somebody relinquished.

The American sense of humor being what it is, Boots was soon running out to the landing strip wearing a small helmet and goggles, complete with an oxygen mask and earphones (made from elements taken from airplane microphones and rigged into the helmet by the base radio technician), and to cap it all off, his own parachute, salvaged from one of the silk drop chutes used for dropping supplies to forward troops.

At five one morning, the big engines of the planes were being warmed up by the flight engineers. The air crews were sipping a second cup of coffee, and the planes that had been loaded the night before were ready for the day's missions. Jeeps carried crews (and Boots) to the planes, and as fast as the tower could clear them, the big C-47 Dakotas were airborne and winging their way deep into Japanese-held Burma.

A C-47 carries no armament, as it is only a transport plane. It's considered a "sitting duck" by enemy aircraft. One plane became separated from the squadron and was jumped by a Japanese Zero, which came up alongside raking the entire plane with explosive ammunition. One shell landed in the bulkhead behind the radio and exploded, showering the radio operator with spalled metal, badly lacerating his nose and forehead.

The man lost consciousness and slumped forward toward the transmitter. He was bleeding profusely. Boots rushed to him, trying to lick his face. When Boots realized that the man was not reviving, he tried to get help. The nearest help was the flight engineer, now straddling the radio and navigator's desks, his head pressed into the navigator's astrodome, reporting to the pilot possible enemy attacks from the plane's otherwise blind rear section.

Boots's barking and yelping could not be heard over the clatter of enemy fire and the roar of the engines. Boots jumped up and locked his jaws on the engineer's pants leg. "Down, Boots!" the man yelled, kicking his leg to dislodge the dog. Again, Boots latched on and hung there. The engineer shouted, "Crazy mutt!" Looking down, he finally saw the radio operator. He took a brief moment to report to the pilot, then came to the operator's aid, administering the necessary first aid.

Did Boot's action measure up as an act of heroism? The wounds sustained by the radio operator proved superficial, so life was not at stake, although Boots didn't know it. Was Boots's life in jeopardy as a result of his act of bravery? Possibly. The engineer was kicking his leg with sufficient strength to dislodge the dog, and Boots could have been slammed against a metal bulkhead.

Heroism? Ask the radio operator. He saw to it that there was one more piece of regalia hanging from Boots's jacket. Boots was, at a formal ceremony, unofficially awarded the Air Medal.

When you start looking for stories of animals in war, you hear thousands of yarns that simply can't be documented, although the tellers will assure you that they are the gospel truth, related firsthand from an unimpeachable source. Some of the stories are so farfetched that it is difficult to believe them. And others are so touching that, true or not, they bear retelling.

The following story is one that I believe. Not just because I want to, but because I heard so many versions of it from so many different sources. Depending on whom you're talking to, it took place on Tarawa, Guam, Leyte, or Guadalcanal.

It seems that a lone GI was patrolling a beach. The camp mascot, a mongrel, trotted along at his side, keeping him company. He'd occasionally reach down to pet the dog or toss a stick for the dog to fetch. It was a dark night, but every now and then the moon peeked out from behind the clouds, bathing the white beach in light.

Then some dark, shadowy forms appeared along the edge of the water. Alert now, the soldier brought his rifle to

Port Arms and shouted a challenge. "Who goes there?" In flawless English, one of the forms answered, "It's okay, Joe—a friend." "Advance, friend, and be recognized," he said, more relaxed now that he heard a friendly voice. "Sure, Joe," the voice answered. "Be right there."

The dog had been watching this entire exchange, sitting quietly all through it. Suddenly, the animal leaped to his feet and bounded across ten feet of beach to lock his jaws on the arm of the lead figure. A shot rang out. The GI dropped to the sand, throwing a cartridge into the chamber of his rifle at the same time. The intruders were no longer speaking English, but shouted to each other in Japanese. The dog clung to the man he had felled, and the GI fired three shots in rapid succession at the others on the beach. Finally, the one intruder shook the dog free from his arm and raised a pistol to kill the dog. Another shot from the GI, and the intruder fell dead.

By this time, the shooting had alerted the guard at the next post, who called for the guard officer. The area was promptly lit with floodlights, and two dead Japanese soldiers were found. (The third lived for questioning later, and he insisted that the dog had been their undoing!) Both the dog and the man received commendations as a result of this action.

All GIs are taught first aid, and during World War II, their instructions were to holler "Medic!" if they were wounded in combat. The medical aid man would get to the wounded man as quickly as possible and administer first aid. This first aid, incidentally, was usually a matter of breaking a paper packet of sulpha powder and sprinkling it into and around the wound.

On the night of the Japanese attack on KunMing Airport in China, the cries of "Medic!" were heard during every lull in the attack. It was a protracted attack, seeming never to end. High explosive shells were followed by antipersonnel bombs that scattered deadly shrapnel. Phosphorus bombs spewed flames and started fires. The Japanese Zero fighter planes escorting the bombers spent their excess ammunition in strafing runs over the ground.

The only thing the GIs could do was cower in the foxholes and hope to avoid a direct hit. Not even the medics could leave their foxholes. The bombardment was too severe and too unpredictable, and there was no way to "time" the bursts. It would have been suicidal for any man to leave his foxhole.

Chink was a mixed shepherd-collie who had attached herself to the squadron. During the attack, the medic yelled "Call Chink" and attached packets of sulpha powder and morphine ampules to the dog's shaggy back with strips of adhesive tape. The wounded simply called the dog, who ran from foxhole to foxhole, allowing men to rip off whatever supplies they needed.

Chink was aware that the outfit was under siege, for she made her way to the men by crawling on her belly. At each foxhole, she got a thank-you in the form of a pat on the head, and returned this with a lick from her big, wet tongue.

Nobody can tell exactly when or where it happened, but at some point during the attack, Chink took two large pieces of shrapnel in her hindquarters, rendering one hind leg utterly useless. Yet in spite of this, in spite of the fact that she must have suffered terrible pain, she continued her ministrations until she wasn't needed any longer. The next day, she was found by the clean-up crew. She was lying on her side, more dead than alive, having lost a great deal of blood. She was carried by litter to a makeshift hospital. The shrapnel was removed, and she made a speedy recovery. The government didn't make any sort of award, but Chink was given her own place in the mess hall after that, and someone managed to find a decoration to attach to her collar.

If you've never lived in a jungle, you may not fully understand or appreciate this next story. A jungle is a hot, steaming, living thing. It overpowers man. The jungle is man's enemy. The very plants can be poisonous, and the animals as well. Scorpions and snakes can be deadly in the jungle. There is no place that is friendly in a friendly jungle, and no jungle is friendly.

Vietnam for the most part is jungle, and it was in the

jungle that the most severe fighting during the Viet Nam War occurred.

This story tells of a simple act of raw courage on the part of a rather small mongrel dog.

On patrol through a stretch of jungle, Sgt. Bill Carter led his men through the tangled undergrowth, idly slapping at the insects that hovered about his neck. The dog gamboled about his legs, now ahead, now behind.

The snakes in Vietnam's jungles hang in complete camouflage from the branches of trees and simply drop onto the bodies of victims who pass beneath. Then they kill their prey either by constriction or venom. These reptiles are all but invisible in their natural habitat.

Dogs, however, are color-blind, and camouflage doesn't work against color blindness. The little dog saw the snake half dangling from the branch. Carter was heading directly into the snake's path. The dog darted between the sergeant's legs, causing him to trip. That small fraction of a second may have saved the sergeant's life. For in that instant, the snake dropped. It missed the sergeant entirely, landing in a heap on the ground, and then, befuddled and confused, quickly slithered into the underbrush.

The dog barked, and the sergeant quickly pegged a shot at the snake as it made its way into the brush.

Medals? Rewards? No. All the dog got was a pat on the head and an invitation to share the sergeant's rations at lunch that day.

The following documents are offered by the Quartermaster General, and we feel that they speak well enough for themselves. These are not simply the jottings of a writer attempting to romanticize a story, they are official government documents.

ARMY DOGS IN WORLD WAR II

The remarkable record of achievement established by army dogs trained by the Army Quartermaster Corps for a variety of duties during World War II removed any doubts which may have existed as to their value in time of war.

Dogs donated by a patriotic public and others purchased by the army saved lives of a number of men in combat. They were instrumental in preventing ambush while operating with patrols and giving warning of enemy infiltration at night. They also performed valuable service in guarding various installations and were used extensively in patrolling the coasts of the United States.

While many of the dogs of World War II have long since been returned to owners, the rapidity with which members of the K-9 Corps responded to training and put that training to excellent use in combat areas is a unique and interesting phase of war history. (NOTE: The widely used phrase K-9 Corps is a popular title for the army's dogs and has even found wide informal usage in the army. The term, however, is not official. Its origin, obviously, is its phonetic association with the words "canine corps.")

Use Of Dogs In War

The extraordinary characteristics of the dog—acuteness of his senses, docility, affection for man, watchfulness, and speed—have enabled him to be of great value for military purposes for many years.

Ancient Greek warriors made use of large dogs, thought by some to be the prototype of the modern mastiff. Romans drafted the same species for attack work, recognizing them as a definite army unit. During the Middle Ages war dogs often received the same complement of armor as did heavyweight chargers and were frequently used to defend large convoys.

Dogs were used as messengers by the army of Frederick the Great. Napoleon himself urged one of his generals to employ them as outposts in the Egyptian campaign at the end of the eighteenth century. Two centuries earlier, on this side of the Atlantic, they helped the Spaniards conquer Mexico and Peru. The North American Indians early developed the use of dogs for pack and draft work as well as for sentry duty.

Ambulance dogs were used successfully by the Russians during the Russo-Japanese War. The French utilized them as ammunition carriers when they found that the strong Pyrenean type could carry as many as five hundred cartridges in a single load. The Bulgarians conscripted their sheep dogs during the Balkan upheaval in 1910 and the Italians in 1911 sent some of their shaggy, white-coated Maremma sheep dogs to Tripoli, where they were picketed in sand dugouts a few hundred yards ahead of the sentries in order to warn of enemy activity.

During World War I the Germans used up to thirty thousand messenger and ambulance dogs. The French used them for more varied work, and to what extent is shown by the fact that when the time came for demobilization in 1919, they had to dispose of more than fifteen thousand. Both the French and Belgian armies used draft dogs, and during the severe winter of 1915 some four hundred sledge dogs were brought from Canada.

When World War II broke out, the French army at once opened recruiting stations for army dogs. Prior to the war Germany had conducted war dog trials under a set of nationally uniform rules. During the fighting in France dogs were used by the Germans for patrol work. The Japanese employed dogs in China. The British during World War II used messenger dogs, patrol dogs, and sentry dogs.

Dogs Used By U.S. Army In World War II

During the war, five War Dog Reception and Training centers were established by the Quartermaster Corps. These were located at Front Royal, Virginia; Fort Robinson, Nebraska; Gulfport, Mississippi; Camp Rimini at Helena, Montana; and San Carlos, California.

Initially training was limited to dogs for sentry work. Later it was expanded to include scout, messenger, sledge and pack dogs, and dogs for use in connection with mine detection. Using dogs for mine detection did not prove feasible, however, and this phase of the program was subsequently abandoned.

27

A little over nineteen thousand dogs, most of which were donated, were processed through the training centers. About 45 percent of these canines were rejected as unsuited for training.

Dogs actually trained and assigned to duty were as follows: Messenger, 151; Scout, 595; Mine Detecting, 140; Sentry, 9,298; Sledge and Pack, 268.

Many different breeds were tried out initially. Later the list was narrowed down to German shepherd, Belgian sheepdog, Doberman pinscher, the farm-type collie and Giant schnauzer. The German shepherd proved to be the most satisfactory.

Start Of The K-9 Corps

Official recognition by the army that dogs could be used for military purposes came on March 13, 1942, when the Quartermaster General was authorized to formulate a program. In July 1942, after three months of studies, surveys, and planning, the Quartermaster Corps formally inaugurated the program and established the first War Dog Reception and Training Center at the Quartermaster Remount Depot, Front Royal, Virginia.

The Quartermaster General was charged with the responsibility of receiving, conditioning, training, and issuance of dogs for all war purposes, as well as of military personnel assigned to such activities. In executing this responsibility the Quartermaster General was also authorized to develop doctrine concerning all phases of this work.

Dogs put into training at the training centers became known as members of the K-9 corps.

At the outset of the program, dogs were secured for the Quartermaster Corps by public donation through Dogs for Defense, Inc., a nonprofit civilian agency created especially for the purpose. This organization, whose members served without pay, had liaison representatives throughout the United States who accepted donations of dogs and arranged for their inspection and shipment to the appropriate army camp.

When the program started, the Quartermaster Corps trained war dogs not only for the army but also for the Marine Corps and Coast Guard. Later these branches procured and trained their own dogs.

By 1943, thousands of sentry dogs had been assigned to duty at war plants, military installations, and with Coast Guard shore patrols. An experimental unit consisting of six scout and two messenger dogs and their handlers was dispatched to the Pacific Area for trials with combat units. Working successfully with both the army and the Marine Corps, taking part both in land campaigns and in landing operations, the satisfactory work of the first dog platoon paved the way for those that were to follow.

Personnel

Extreme care was exercised in selecting military personnel to help in the training of dogs for duty.

Men were trained at the dog reception and training centers after being carefully interviewed as to their qualifications for this specialized type of work. Emphasis was placed on a friendly attitude toward dogs, intelligence, patience and perseverance, mental and physical coordination, physical endurance, resourcefulness, and dependability in selecting personnel to handle the dogs.

Qualified veterinarians were assigned to provide for the care of the canines.

Tattooing

A day following the arrival of a dog at the reception and training center, a careful record was made concerning the canine's background. The veterinarian then tattooed the dog's assigned number on the left ear, on the flank, or on the belly, for purposes of identification.

At the training centers, war dogs began a rigid military routine. Close attention was given to grooming and care, and the diet was carefully regulated.

A basic training period was initiated during which the dog was trained to carry out certain fundamental commands. These included, while on a leash, to obey such commands as heel, sit, down, cover, stay, come, crawl, and jump. Off the leash the dog was trained to drop and jump. He was also accustomed to muzzles, gas masks, riding in a variety of vehicles, and to gunfire. Some dogs were also transported by plane with little trouble.

The basic training served to develop in dogs behavior that was basic to a more specialized training for specific military functions, as well as to determine the function for which each dog might be best suited. It was learned early that a dog might be trained for scout, messenger, or sentry work, but that he could not satisfactorily combine two or more duties of this type.

Specialized training varied with the type of work for which the dog was being fitted.

The sentry dog worked on a short leash and was taught to give warning by growling, alerting, or barking. He was especially valuable for working in the dark when attack from cover or the rear was most likely.

Scout or patrol dogs also worked on a leash, day and night, in all kinds of weather and over all types of terrain. Above all, their training provided for working in silence in order to aid the detecting of snipers, ambushes, and other enemy forces in a particular locality.

Messenger dogs were trained to work with two handlers, learning to make their own way upon being unleashed from one handler to the other. Taught to travel silently and by a circuitous route if necessary, the messenger dog soon became adept at taking advantage of natural cover and bypassing any group except the one that included his handler.

Battle conditioning, of course, was a necessary part of dog training. The canine was taught to be oblivious of all things that did not interfere with a given mission. The orientation course began with the firing of a rifle at a distance while the dog was engaged in regular activity. As the dog became more accustomed to this type of sound, he eventually came to pay little or no attention to fire of small arms or larger weapons.

Most dogs were trained in a matter of twelve weeks. The sentry dog, however, usually completed his course in eight weeks.

Training was conducted by the handler who would be with the dog in the field, under the supervision of expert instructors.

Equipment

Standard dog equipment included two collars—a leather kennel collar and a chain collar—web harness, a leash, a kennel chain, a muzzle, water-repellent blanket, brush and comb, individual feeding and watering pans, and gas masks.

Evaluation of War Dog Program

Although the results of much of the war dog program during World War II were negative, these undoubtedly were outweighed by the positive results. The best evidence of this was the fact that the War Department authorized scout dog platoons in the postwar Military Establishment. For the first time in its history the army recognized that dogs possessed sufficient tactical value to justify their inclusion among the regular peacetime units.

Recognition of War Dogs

A number of war dogs trained by the Quartermaster Corps established outstanding records overseas. At least one member of the K-9 Corps was awarded the Silver Star and the Purple Heart by an overseas command. Both were later revoked as contrary to army policy which prohibited official commendation for outstanding performance by animals. In January 1944, the War Department relaxed restrictions in this regard, however, and permitted publication of commendations in individual unit General Orders. Later approval was granted for issuance by the Quartermaster General of citation certificates to donors of war dogs that had been unusually helpful during the war. The first issued were in recognition of the work of eight dogs comprising the first experimental unit in the Pacific Area.

Some Outstanding Dogs

TEDDY, Brand Number T115. In October 1943 the War Dog Unit of which Teddy was a member was reassigned to a marine raider regiment of the Sixth Army. Traveling by plane, the dog and his handler went to another staging area. In December, the Raiders moved to Finschafen to take part in the Cape Gloucester operations in the South Pacific. The entire dog detachment went ashore with the first wave and figured prominently in the operations. Until March, the dog was used continuously for patrol and messenger work. Lines were gradually extended to make contact with the army forces near Gilnit. In these weeks, there was not a single instance in which any of the dogs failed to accomplish a mission, nor was there an instance when a patrol led by a war dog was fired upon first or suffered casualties. In contrast, dogless patrols suffered casualties, usually as a result of ambush or surprise attacks. During this period, the patrols led by dogs were officially credited with 180 Japanese casualties and 20 prisoners.

SANDY, Brand Number B11. Sandy was a natural selection for messenger training. Handled by Sgt. Guy C. Sheldon and Sgt. Menzo J. Brown, yeoman service was contributed throughout the Cape Gloucester campaign. His outstanding performance was carried out during the advance on the airstrip. Near Turzi Point, the advance units were held up by Japanese pillboxes and fortifications and aid of the artillery could not be sought by the walkie-talkies which were temporarily out of commission. A message was dispatched by Sergeant Brown back to the Battalion Command Post through Sandy. Although the dog had not seen Sergeant Sheldon since the night before and he was then in a new location, Sandy unerringly found his way to Sergeant Sheldon's foxhole. The dog had to travel through the tall kunai grass, swim a river, and for part of the distance make his way beneath a curtain of mortar and tank fire, and finally jump a barbed wire fence that protected Sergeant Sheldon. As a result of this message, artillery fire was directed on the Japanese defenses, pulverizing them and permitting the American forward units to resume their advance.

DICK, Brand Number T127. Dick and his handler, Sgt. Herman H. Boude, patrolled 48 days out of 53 and scarcely a day passed without his alerting to Japanese in numbers varying from single stragglers attempting to rejoin their units to entire platoons. In no instance did Dick fail to warn of the enemy in time to allow him to be either killed or captured in a surprise attack. Once while on patrol, the scouting party was warned of the enemy's presence by Dick's alerting; by quartering, the patrol discovered a camouflaged bivouac of five huts indicating it to be the only inhabited one. This proved to be the case when a surprise attack was made in which four Japanese were annihilated without a single casualty.

BOBO, Brand Number Z303. Bobo and his handler, Sgt. John Coleman, led a reconnaisance patrol safely into German-held territory. Their mission accomplished, the patrol started back to their own lines. Scarcely a hundred yards from the outpost, Bobo alerted sharply and definitely straight ahead, then to the left, then to the right. A German patrol was in the act of surrounding the outpost, so a scout was sent on to warn the men who were holding it. The enemy was dispersed, and the patrol proceeded back to headquarters.

SILVER, Brand Number A595. Silver was killed in action 17 February 1945 in a foxhole by an enemy hand grenade. She was responsible for preventing serious casualties by alerting prior to a bayonet attack.

PEEFKE, Brand Number T133. Peefke was killed in action by a direct hit from an enemy hand grenade on 20 March 1945. Members of the patrol on which he was killed commended him highly. Prior to his death on this patrol he discovered a wire and alerted his handler, who, upon examination of the wire, found three enemy "S" mines, which were then neutralized. These mines, had they not been discovered, could have caused grave damage to the patrol. Peefke performed faithful service throughout his tour of duty.

PAL, Brand Number 8M2. Pal was killed by enemy action on 23 April 1945 at San Benedetto Po, Italy. In blocking a shrapnel charge with his own body, Pal prevented the serious wounding of several men. His body absorbed the shrapnel destined to wipe out the advance patrol.

BUSTER, Brand Number A684. While operating as a messenger dog with "F" Company, 155th Infantry Regiment, on Morotai Island, Buster was directly responsible for saving the lives of an entire patrol consisting of seventeen men. His determined effort carried him through heavy enemy machine gun and mortar fire on a total of two trips, bringing instructions for the patrol to hold its position at all costs. He was thus responsible for reinforcements which accounted for the destruction of an entire enemy force.

BRUCE, Brand Number T178. During a banzai attack occurring in Northern Luzon at 0315 hours on 17 February 1945 against "E" Company, 27th Infantry, Bruce, without command, voluntarily attacked three Japanese infantrymen advancing with fixed bayonets toward a foxhole containing two wounded American soldiers. By his fearless action the lives of the two wounded men were saved; by discouraging the advance of these particular Japanese, more casualties were averted.

WOLF, Brand Number T121. Wolf was committed to combat with the 27th Infantry battling through the Corabello Mountains in northern Luzon toward the strategic Balete Pass. While leading an infantry patrol he scented the presence of the enemy entrenched on a hillside about 150 yards distant in time to allow the members of the patrol to take favorable cover and resist the attack that was imminent. During the ensuing firefight, Wolf received shrapnel wounds. Showing no sign of pain and determined at all costs to remain silent, his wound was not detected by surrounding personnel. Greatly outnumbered and partly encircled by the enemy, the patrol decided to withdraw to insure the delivery to headquarters of the vital information they had gained. Wolf, on the point of the patrol, succeeded on three different occasions in alerting the patrol, enabling them to bypass the enemy and return to their camp without a single casualty. In spite of expert medical care and an emergency operation, the 25th division's casualty list included, among others—Wolf, US Army War Dog, T121, Died of Wounds, Wounded in action.

DUCHESS, Brand Number 7H74. Duchess was a member of the 39th Infantry Scout Dog Platoon. On April 1945, Duchess, handled by Sergeant Knight, on patrol with the 3rd Batallion, 123rd Infantry, was used in the inspection of enemy cave installations on Luzon in the Philippines. On approaching a large one, the dog was permitted to go to the entrance. At this point she gave a strong alert. Grenades were thrown into the cave, after which the patrol moved on. Investigation the following day revealed thirty-three Japanese dead in the cave.

On another occasion, Duchess and Sergeant Knight were on patrol with the same unit. Duchess alerted on some Filipino huts, eight hundred yards away. Investigation disclosed the presence of enemy. Mortar and machine gun fire were used to kill nine Japanese.

BLACKIE, Brand Number H24. On 12 and 13 April 1945, while on a two-day patrol with Company F, 123rd Infantry, Blackie, handled by Corporal Technician Kido, was used alternately on that point. The patrol successfully completed its mission without detection by the enemy, locating an area where 500 Japanese were bivouacked. As patrol was on the reconnaissance, all contact with the enemy was avoided.

Returning War Dogs to Civilian Life

When World War II hostilities ended, the Quartermaster Corps put into operation a well-conceived plan for return of war dogs to their civilian owners. No dog, it was announced, would be considered ready for release by the army until it had undergone a complete "demilitarizing" process.

When a dog was considered surplus to army needs, it was immediately transferred to a reprocessing section for rehabilitation to civilian life. Its past record was carefully studied, for such a study often revealed how best to approach it. Handlers made a point of convincing the dog that every human being is a friend. If he were inclined to romp, they played with him. If he were suspicious, they talked to him gently. A dog that is not under control is difficult to handle. For this reason, every time a dog was taken from his kennel during the demilitarizing process he was made to "heel" properly and respond to commands to "sit," to " down," and to "stay." Before a dog was returned he was thoroughly grounded in this type of obedience training.

An accurate record was kept of the daily progress of each dog, and when reaction was favorable over a period of time, he was subjected to different tests. While working in a group of other dogs, for example, he might be subjected to gunfire, having people ride around him on bicycles, or be placed in an area where there was a great deal of noise. Passing such tests as these indicated a readiness for return to civilian life.

More freedom was given the dog as each test was passed successfully. He was permitted to run and frolic at the end of a thirty-foot exercise leash and subjected to handling by men in civilian clothes. As one of the final tests, an element of surprise was introduced. The dog was walked on leash by a secluded building. As he passed the building, an aggravator jumped at him from behind, waving a sack and shouting. If the dog showed no unusual alarm and readily tried to make friends with the aggravator, it was felt that he had earned the right to return to civilian life. Before being shipped, every canine was given a final check by a veterinary officer.

THE KOREAN CONFLICT

Use of Dogs in Combat

Before the outbreak of hostilities in Korea, the army was using dogs in Seoul for sentry duty around warehouses and storage areas. More than one hundred dogs were stationed there and their work proved extremely beneficial in reducing theft and pilferage.

When fighting began in Korea, there was one Infantry scout dog platoon in training at Fort Riley, Kansas, which was sent over there to assist combat patrols. This platoon, the 26th, saw almost continuous service and opened the eyes of many regimental commanders to the potential value of dogs attached to patrols. One regimental commander remarked that after using a dog for a while patrols did not want to go out without them. This one platoon was not capable of spreading itself thin enough to fill the demand.

The 26th infantry Scout Dog Platoon was cited in General Orders, Department of the Army, No. 21, 27 February 1953, as follows:

> The 26th Infantry Scout Dog Platoon is cited for exceptionally meritorious conduct in the performance of outstanding services in direct support of combat operations in Korea during the period 12 June 1951 to 15 January 1953. The 26th Infantry Scout Dog Platoon, during its service in Korea, has participated in hundreds of combat patrol actions by supporting the patrols with the services of an expert scout dog handler and his highly trained scout dog. The members of the 26th Infantry Scout Dog Platoon, while participating in these patrols, were invariably located at the most vulnerable points in the patrol formation in order that the special aptitudes of the trained dog could be most advantageously used to give warning of the presence of the enemy. The unbroken record of faithful and gallant performance of these missions by the individual handlers and their dogs in support of patrols has saved countless casualties through giving early warning to the friendly patrol of threats to its security. The full value of the services rendered by the 26th Infantry Scout Dog Platoon is nowhere better understood and more highly recognized than among the members of the patrols with whom the scout dog handlers and their dogs have operated. When not committed to action, the soldiers of the 26th Infantry Scout Dog Platoon have given unfailing efforts to further developing their personal skills as well as that of their dogs in order to better perform the rigorous duties which are required of them while on patrol. Throughout its long period of difficult and hazardous service, the 26th Infantry Scout Dog Platoon has never failed those with whom it served, has consistently shown outstanding devotion to duty in the performance of all of its other duties, and has won on the battlefield a degree of respect and admiration which has established it as a unit of the greatest importance to the Eighth United States Army. The outstanding

performance of duty, proficiency, and esprit de corps invariably exhibited by the personnel of this platoon reflect the greatest credit on themselves and the military service of the United States.

(General Orders 114, Headquarters, Eighth United States Army, Korea, 18 January 1953).

As a result of the outstanding service rendered by the 26th Infantry Scout Dog Platoon, recommendation was made and approved for the activation of a scout dog platoon to be attached to each division in Korea, but the war reached the "peace talks" stage before five additional platoons were trained and shipped to Korea.

Sentry dogs were used by the army and the air force for guarding bases and supply points in Korea, Japan, and Okinawa. The psychological effect of the dogs' presence is difficult to estimate yet the fact remains that innumerable individuals have reported that when a dog and handler were assigned to an area, pilferage stopped. When the conflict was over, scout dogs not assigned to Infantry Divisions were retrained for sentry work.

Dogs, of course, are an important part of military life even today. In recognition of their courage, dedication, and service, *Army Digest* magazine ran the following story in February 1967.

THE ARMY'S FOUR-FOOTED SENTRIES

Dogged Persistence

When his handler, PFC William Richardson, was wounded, scout dog Troubles wasn't allowed in the helicopter that carried the soldier to a hospital ten miles away at An Khe. But three weeks after the episode, Troubles was found back at the 1st Air Cavalry Division head-quarters—thin, tired, and refusing to let anybody come near him. He made his way to the scout dog platoon, searched through the tents until he found the one containing

PFC Richardson's equipment, climbed into the bunk, and settled down there. Just how he managed to find his way back is a mystery to the dog trainers, since there was no trail or scent to follow. Troubles and his master had been airlifted into the jungle.

A new breed of fighter has arrived in the Republic of Vietnam. The reaction of the United States units fighting there has been no less than enthusiastic. Here are some comments:

"He works easy," says Sergeant Castle of the 3d Brigade Task Force, 25th Infantry Division. "He's got a good nose. He'll find anything if it's out there."

"Once the men get accustomed to working with them, we'll really have a rough team going against Charlie," says Sergeant First Class Arthur Porter of the 38th Infantry Platoon, 2d Batallion, 27th Infantry, 25th Infantry Division.

From the 3d Platoon of C Company, 2d Batallion, 12th Cavalry, 1st Air Cavalry Division, comes more enthusiastic praise: "Duke really worked out great. He found enemy grenades, rice, clothing, and small arms ammunition."

The army isn't going to the dogs but the dogs are going to the army, and their recent arrival in Vietnam has brought forth this high praise. After serving well in past wars, the scout dog is being put to use again in Vietnam. The dogs are used for several types of operations including combat and reconnaissance patrols, sweeping operations, village clearing missions, and security. Their noses are keyed to detect ambushers, buried mines, and trip wires.

There are now several dog platoons with units in Vietnam. The first assigned to the 1st Cavalry Division was such a success that others have joined the 1st and 25th Infantry Divisions.

After initial training at Fort Benning, where they went through three months of training in the fields and swamps of Georgia, the dogs and their handlers received additional training upon arrival in Vietnam.

The association between the dog and his handler is

all-important in determining how effective a team will be. Each handler knows his dog—that his canine companion won't bark while on patrol, that he can smell forty times better, hear twenty times better and see ten times better than a man. Even in bad weather, the dog can smell a Viet Cong one hundred yards away and can pick up a scent five hundred yards distant when the wind is right.

The average age of the dog entering training is two and a half years. He'll be good for seven more years—if he lives that long. The Viet Cong have orders to aim for the dog first and then his handler—the scout dog teams have been that effective in Vietnam.

Dogs and handlers must learn each other's traits. The dogs—mostly German shepherds—will show alertness in differing ways. One might turn his head in the direction of the scent or sound while another might just prick up his ears or tug at the leash. This is only one reason why a particular soldier always works with the same animal.

When the dog "alerts" on a patrol, the handler puts up his hand and stops. He bends down behind his dog and with arms outstretched indicates the spot his dog has detected. Then he moves to the rear of the patrol and leaves the rest to the infantry.

Another good reason for having a dog along on patrol in a war in which mines and booby traps produce a high percentage of casualties is that the dogs will alert at any suspicious object on the trail. The platoon leader of the 38th Scout Dog Platoon with the 25th Division pointed out the value. "Our best trained dogs won't cross a trip wire, even if they're ordered to move on. The dog will go from one end of the wire to the other but he won't cross it."

Before going on a mission, the handler introduces his dog to the men of the patrol. The dog gets a chance to familiarize himself with the smell of the men so that he will not give false alerts on friendly troops. If a handler is wounded, the dog will usually permit himself to be led by one of the men he had previously met.

The dogs aren't immune from any type of duty; they go

41

where their handlers go. If a mission requires a parachute jump, the dog goes along. Future plans envision using the dogs for tunnel running—ferreting out Viet Cong in underground hideaways. It may not be long before the tunnel rat gives way to the canine tunnel puppy.

Dogs have been a part of war for centuries. The Romans put spiked collars around their necks and sent them against the enemy as fighters. The Germans used dogs extensively during both World Wars, mustering some two hundred thousand in World War II. The Japanese also used dogs in World War II, and the Viet Cong are using dogs today. The U.S. employed dogs about two years after World War II began under a program called Dogs for National Defense. The use of dogs during the Korean War was especially effective.

To the time-honored declaration that a dog is man's best friend, veterans of combat patrols in the Republic of Vietnam add a solemn "amen."

While dogs naturally figure prominently in any stories of heroism, they are by no means alone.

Consider the navy flier who was shot down in combat by enemy aircraft. Before bailing out of the damaged plane, he radioed his position, then parachuted into what he thought would be the relative safety of the sea until air-sea rescue could come to his aid. Following proper procedure, he released the chute when he was about ten feet over the surface of the waves. He fell into the water as the wind blew the limp parachute aside. He tugged at the two gas cartridges to inflate his life vest. Pulling at another tab, he released the dye marker that would pinpoint his location for the search plane and started the automatic transponder that sent out a radio beam. Bobbing helplessly on the surface, he wondered if his leg wound was very severe. He knew it was bleeding.

What he saw next sent a cold shiver down his spine: a triangle-shaped fin that could only mean a shark. He tugged at the shark-repellant flap and flailed at the surface of the water, but he really felt doomed, for he knew sharks were able to detect even a tiny trace of blood in the water.

As he watched, additional fins appeared, hurtling toward him. It was only a matter of time until he fell prey to the sharp teeth.

Then a strange thing happened. The waters churned, and the sharks appeared to be fighting with each other. The other fins did not belong to sharks but to porpoises, who now attacked the sharks ruthlessly. Again and again, the porpoises turned to attack, driving their blunt snouts into the sharks' sides with such force as to drive the breath out of the sharks' lungs and break the bones of their rib cages. The waters were bloodied, but this time with the blood of the sharks as they succumbed to the porpoise attack.

As the last sharks were driven off, the porpoises swam in circles around the downed flier, protecting him against further attack.

Before long, the big PBY appeared and made a landing on the water. A lifeline and ring were tossed to the flier. He was quickly hauled aboard the plane, which transported him to a land-based hospital where his wounds were treated.

The records are replete with other stories relating how porpoises, also called dolphins, have aided man.

One navy flier in the South Pacific sustained heavy damage to his plane in combat and knew he'd never make it back to his base. The engine was smoking profusely, so he radioed that he was going to ditch and gave his position. The base radioed that help would soon be on the way.

He followed the standard ditching procedure. He jettisoned the plastic canopy to ease his escape, then set up his approach. At the last minute, he cut the engine and held the plane in a nose-high stall attitude. The plane dropped to the surface of the sea, and then, with a lurch, settled. Quickly, the pilot inflated the orange-colored life raft and clambered aboard, paddling as far from the sinking plane as he could, so he would not be sucked down into the vortex created by the drowning aircraft.

He watched as the big plane was slowly swallowed by the lapping waves, and then he rested, awaiting his rescue.

That was when the group of porpoises appeared. They squawked encouraging greetings, and began bumping the raft one after another, pushing the raft slowly but inexorably toward an island that was nearby.

What did porpoises know of man and his wars? Nothing at all. But the pilot knew. That island was occupied by the enemy.

There he was, helpless at sea, knowing that his rescue was scant minutes away, and the porpoises were pressing him closer and closer to the enemy. Taking the paddle, the flier began beating at the porpoises as they tried to help him. As each porpoise came in to give the raft another push, he swung the paddle at the animal, trying to dissuade the assistance it offered. The porpoises did not understand, and this crazy battle went on for nearly half an hour before help finally arrived.

The pilot was exhausted from fighting this unwanted assistance when he was finally taken aboard the rescue plane. However, he did leave the raft for the porpoises to play with!

One rarely thinks of birds as heroic, but during World War I, in France, carrier pigeons performed many important actions. The carrier pigeon has but one thought in mind, and that is to return to the nest. If you take a carrier from his nest, then release him, he will fly back by the most direct means possible. If you attach a message to his leg, the message will surely get back along with the bird. The bird's singleness of purpose is caused only by his instinctive need to return home. (Actually, the term "carrier pigeon" is a biological misnomer. "Carrier" is merely a descriptive term. All the "carrier" pigeons used by the army were, biologically speaking, homing pigeons.)

Harry was a carrier pigeon who was taken to the front along with a company of soldiers. When the outfit was under siege and desperately needed artillery support and medical aid, a message was hastily scrawled and fitted to the small cannister attached to Harry's leg. Harry was lifted at arm's length from the trenches and released. With a flurried beating of his wings, Harry gained altitude, circled once, and headed for home.

The enemy soldiers were no fools. They knew that a carrier pigeon had been released, for they could easily see the white bird as it flew. To prevent the delivery of the important message, they shot at the bird.

Any hunter can tell you that it is useless to go after fowl with a rifle. A scatter-gun is used. But the desperate soldiers, not having shotguns, fired rifles at the hapless bird, and Harry succumbed to a lucky shot that drove through his wing. Unbalanced and disabled, he plummeted to the earth.

Harry did not die. The wind was knocked out of him by his fall. His wing, though broken, was miraculously still partially usable. He persevered, and—albeit a good deal later than anyone had planned, several days later, in fact—Harry appeared at the hutch back at the base camp. The message was delivered, and the day—finally—was saved.

Probably the most celebrated pigeon of all time is Cher Ami, which means "dear friend" in French. The bird was also known, according to some military reports, as Big Tom. Cher Ami was labeled a Black Check Cock in some reports, a Blue Check Hen in others. There is also some confusion regarding the awards given this bird. It has been stated that Cher Ami received the Distinguished Service Medal from the United States and the Croix de Guerre from France. However, while strict search has been made, no documentation for either award can be found.

A bit of romantic confusion also surrounds his exploits with the so-called Lost Batallion of World War I. (Army fact sheets tell us that this was not actually a batallion but a unit made up of several infantry and machine gun companies.)

During the Meuse-Argonne campaign, the troops of the Lost Batallion were completely surrounded by enemy forces from October 3 until October 7. They were never really "lost," for they held their ground until the main lines could be brought up to relieve them.

Let's pick up here with a story printed in the *New York World* on Sunday, May 26, 1929.

ANIMAL HEROES

On the morning of October 2, 1918, that never-to-be-forgotten morning, a general advance was ordered in the Argonne. The 77th Division was directed to take and hold certain forward positions, regardless of cost or loss. The objectives were fixed and the word was given. Late that afternoon six companies of the 306th, one of the 307th, and two machine gun companies of the 305th, under Major Whittlesey, reached their objective, dug in, and threw out advance listening posts. On the morrow they awoke to find that the forces on both their flanks had been driven back and that they were surrounded by the Germans, with their communications entirely cut off. Here they were, 554 men with only one day's rations.

In the storm of German fire and the barrage of the American artillery which swept back and forth across their location, they lost twenty-five percent of their men the first day. There was no surgeon or medical officer with them, and only two first-aid men. They had no means of caring properly for the wounded and the dying. Volunteer after volunteer started through the enemy lines, only to be killed or captured. One by one the little force sent out six of its seven carrier pigeons, only to see most of them picked off by German marksmen. Hourly the slaughter went on.

On the third day it looked as though all hope was gone. The American artillery was working terrible havoc upon this lost battalion of its own army. There was but one pigeon left, and that was Cher Ami. The officers of the lost battalion wrote this message: "For God's sake, lift the fire!", added the little force's location, and put the scrap of paper in the aluminum carrier on the pigeon's leg. Then in that death ridden air they released their last bird—their final hope.

Cher Ami took off like a shot. The soldier watched breathlessly. The bird was hit. They saw the valiant flyer falter and plunge to the ground. What they thought, no man can write! But the bird was up again—up and away! Some voice had called, it seemed, and Cher Ami heard—"Cher Ami, come home."

A short time later Cher Ami fluttered down on the roof of the pigeon loft at Rampont, little more than a blood-smeared fluff of feathers. One of his wings was shot through, one leg was gone—he carried the message dangling from its ligaments. But he had saved the Lost Battalion, or what remained of it. For the Americans advanced and succeeded in bringing back 194 of Major Whittlesey's command.

Now the transport *Ohioan* brought Cher Ami, his wounds more or less healed, back to America on April 16, 1919. Not only did General Pershing hold him in his hand before the ship sailed, but he ordered that the Argonne hero should be lodged in a pigeon officer's cabin en route. Home, everyone wanted to see Cher Ami. To cap the climax, Cher Ami was kept in Washington as the mascot of the Signal Corps and on recommendation of General E. E. Russell he was awarded the Distinguished Service Medal. Cher Ami deid in Forth Monmouth, New Jersey, in 1919. He was mounted and is now on display in the National Museum in Washington.

The full impact of Cher Ami's heroism emerges when you read the actual messages transmitted by Major Whittlesey from his entrapped position.

The following are the messages received via Pigeon service at Columbier Fixo #66, Les Senados, Argonne Sector, France, from 308th Infantry, 77th Division, U.S.A., Major Charles W. Whittlesey, Commanding Officer.

#1 Headquarters of C.O., 1st Bn. to C.O. 308th Inf.

Our runner posts seem to have broken down during the night as we have received no word from you. Have sent Adjutant 1st Bn. to re-establish route. It was O.K. till 9 P.M. yesterday.

We have not heard from patrols to 4 Cos. of this Regt. on East of Ravine. Have just sent another patrol of our best men to find them.

Will await orders here for the time being. In any event will either stay here or advance.

Place 94.8-74.5 Sept. 29, 1918

                    (signed) Whittlesey.
Released 7:02 A.M. Arrived 12:38 N.

#2 Headquarters of C.O., 1st Bn., 308th Inf. to C.O. 308th Inf.

Our line of communication with the rear is still cut at 12:30 P.M. by German M-guns. We are now going to clean out one of these guns. From a wounded German Officer prisoner we learn there is a German Company of 70 operating in our rear to close the gap we made yesterday. We can, of course, clean up this country to the rear by working our companies back over the ground we came. But we understood our mission is to advance, and to maintain our strength here; and it is very slow trying to clear up this rear area from here by small details, when this trickling sack of M-guns can be repeated by the enemy indefinitely. Can this line of communication not be kept open by a unit from the rear?

We are not yet in touch with the four companies of this Regt. to the East of the Ravine East of here as none of our patrols have yet returned.

The closing up of the 1st and 2nd Bns. was necessitated by yesterday's operation, and the splitting of the Echelons by the Ravine East of here. Major Budd collaborates in these reports.

Place 94.8-74.5 Sept. 29, 1918
Released 1:09 P.M. Arrived 1:17 P.M.
                    (signed) Whittlesey, Major,
                              1st Bn., 308.

#3 Headquarters of C.O., 1st Bn., 308th Inf. to C.O., 308th Inf.

A patrol which we sent to get in touch with

units on our left has just returned, having crossed the R.R. tracks S.W. of here, and reached a point approximately 294-273.5. Germans, including 2 officers, were seen at the point, and others along the way. No Americans were met.

We have killed a German officer who was scouting here (94.8-74.5) this morning, also killed one other German and taken a wounded prisoner. We have seen about 20 others passing thru the woods near here. From the officer we have taken some valuable maps.

We have not been able to keep open our lines of communication owing to German M-guns which have filtered thru in our rear or come in from the West; and we shall not be able to do so without abandoning part of our position which we hesitate to do, as we understand our mission to be to advance.

We have sent 3 pigeon messages today asking that our lines of communication be kept open by units from our rear, that we may get food and ammunition.

Place 94.8-74.5 Sept. 29, 1918.
Released 4:00 P.M. Arrived 4:26 P.M.
(signed) Whittlesey, Major,
308th Inf.

#4 Headquarters of C.O., 1st Bn., 308th Inf. to C.O., 308th Inf.
We are being shelled by German Artillery.
Can we not have artillery support.
This is coming from NORTHWEST.

Place 294.6-276.3 Oct. 3, 1918.
Released 8:50 A.M. Arrived 9:25 A.M.
(signed) Whittlesey, Major
308th

49

#5 Headquarters of C.O., 1st Bn., 308th Inf. to C.O., 308th Infty.

Our runner posts are broken. One runner captured. Germans in small numbers are working to our left rear about 294.6-276.2. Have sent K Co., 307 to occupy this hill and open the line. Patrols to EAST ran into Germans at 295.1-296.3 (6 Bosches)

Have located German MORTAR at 294.05-276.3 and have sent platoon to get it.

Have taken prisoner who says his company of 70 men were brought in here last night to 294.4-276.2 from the rear by motor trucks. He saw only a few infantrymen here when he came in.

German machine gun constantly firing on valley in our rear from hill 294.1-276.

E Co. (sent to meet D&F) met heavy resistance at least 20 casualties, 20 squads under Lt. Leake have just fallen back here.

Place 294.6-276.3 Oct. 3, 1918
Released 10:45 A.M. Arrived 11:27 A.M.
(signed) Whittlesey,
Major, 308th

#6 Headquarters of C.O., 1st Bn., 308th Inf. to C.O., 308th Inf.

Germans are on cliff NORTH of us in small numbers and have tried to envelope both flanks. Situation on left flank very serious.

Broke thru two of our runner posts today near 294.7-275.7. I have not been able to re-establish posts today.

Need 8000 round rifle arms.
7500 Chauchat, 23 boxes M. G.
250 Offensive grenades.

Casualties yesterday in Companies (A,B,C,E,G,H) 8 killed, 80 wounded. In same

Pride, a New York City police horse, received the Certificate of Merit from the ASPCA for courage during an explosion in the Wall Street area. His partner, Officer Eugene Kempton, is on the right.

Mike Zezima of Long Beach, New York, credits Turkey (shown wearing the ASPCA Medal for Honor) with saving his life during a blizzard.

KEN-L-RATION DOG HERO
OF THE YEAR AWARDS

1954 Tang-collie	Denison, Texas
1955 Taffy-cocker spaniel	Coeur d'Alene, Idaho
1956 Lassie-shetland sheepdog	San Carlos, Calif.
1957 Blaze-collie	Timewell, Ill.
1958 Dutchess-German shepherd	Excelsior, Minn.
1959 Lady-collie/German shepherd	Mehlville, Mo.
1960 Keg-German shepherd	Bozeman, Mont.
1961 Duke-collie	Niles, Ohio
1962 Beggar-St. Bernard	Sacramento, Calif.
1963 Dutch-German shepherd	Troy, Pa.
1964 Buddy-collie	Budd Lake, N.J.
1965 Patches-collie/malamute	Spanaway, Wash.
1966 Hero-collie (show dog)	Priest River, Idaho
1967 Mijo-St. Bernard	Anchorage, Alaska
1968 Ringo-part St. Bernard	Euless, Texas
1969 Top-Great Dane	Los Angeles, Calif.
1970 Grizzly Bear-St. Bernard	Denali, Texas
1971 Trixie-mixed	Lynn, Mass.
1972 Mimi-miniature poodle	Danbury, Conn.
1973 Budweiser-St. Bernard	John's Island S.C.
1974 Skippy-mixed	Santa Ana, Calif.
1975 Fawn-German shepherd	St. Petersburg, Fla.
1976 Zorro-German shepherd/wolf	Orangevale, Calif.
1977 Meatball-German shepherd	Morris, Ala.
1978 Chessie-Chesapeake Bay Retriever	Livingston, Mont.

The pictures which follow are of the Dog Heroes of the Year, awarded annually since 1954.

1954-A collie who risked his life to rescue children on at least five separate occasions, Tang is shown here with one of his self-appointed charges.

1955-Stevie Wilson shows his affection for Taffy, whose actions saved the young boy from drowning.

1956-With an act of disobedience Lassie saved her young master, Gary Gustafson, who was in desperate need of medical attention.

1957-Dawn Hecox and Blaze, who rescued the girl after she was attacked by an enraged sow.

1958-Dutchess and Linda Phillippi at Lake William, where
the German shepherd saved the girl from drowning.

1959-Lady, the first mongrel to win, is shown here with young
Tommy Abel.

1961-Duke suffered burns to save Penny Grantz from being enveloped in flames.

1960-Karen McMannis and Keg. The German shepherd rescued Karen from a rushing, flooded creek into which the toddler had fallen.

1962-Bobby Mitchell plays under the watchful eye of the family's St. Bernard, Beggar, who kept the young boy alive when he disappeared from home.

1963-Dutch enjoys the attention of Hugh (r.) and Gordon (l.) Hawthorne, who are alive today as a result of the dog's courage and strength.

1965-Marvin Scott, shown here with Patches, points to the place where the dog rescued him from freezing waters.

1964-In addition to the "Dog Hero of the Year" award, Buddy was named "Businessman's Best Friend" for saving his master's dairy herd from fire.

1966-Hero and Shawn Jolley. The collie suffered numerous injuries in his successful struggle to save Shawn from a crazed horse.

1967-Philiciann Bennett shows her love and gratitude to Mijo, who saved the teenager from drowning.

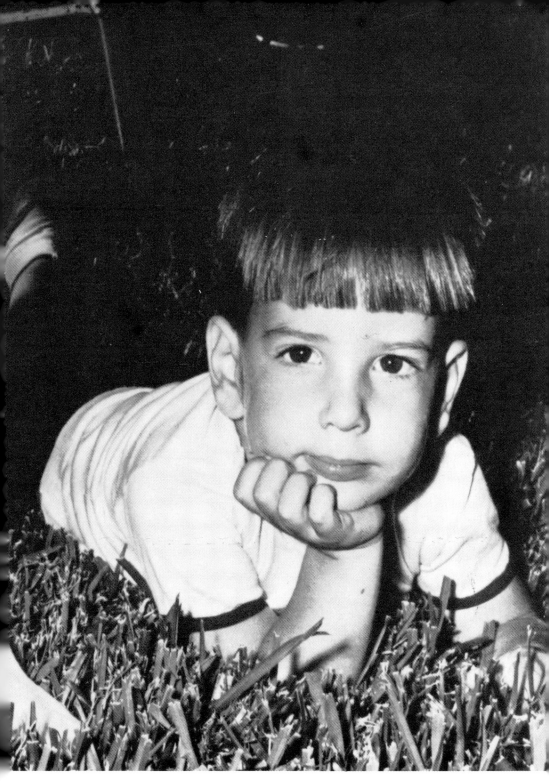

1968-A stray who came to stay, Ringo stopped traffic until Randy Saleh could be rescued from a busy highway.

1969-Top, with his master, Axel Patzwaldt. The Great Dane saved a young child from drowning just weeks after being injured during another rescue.

1970-Mrs. David Gratias proudly displays her dog's Medal of Honor. Grizzley Bear saved his mistress during an attack by a real grizzly.

1971-Ricky Sherry and his dog Trixie share a happy moment.
Trixie's actions saved Ricky from an icy pond.

1972-Size has no bearing on heroism. Mimi's abundant courage and intelligence saved all eight members of the **Emerito** family from a fire.

1974-Donald Essig shows Skippy their picture in the Orange County, California, *Register*. The dog's life was endangered when he fought the rattlesnake that was about to strike at Donald.

1973-Linda Lawson (l.) and Joyce Hinson (r.) with their rescuer. Budweiser pulled both cousins from a burning house.

1975-Russ Schoenberger hugs Fawn, who saved him from a rattlesnake. The German shepherd acted with unusual heroism to protect the young boy.

1976-A camping trip turned disastrous. Without Zorro along, Mark Cooper would have died from injuries and exposure.

1977-Meatball receives a well deserved hug from Mary Evelyn Keith as her parents look on. The German shepherd was injured while trying to catch would-be burglars.

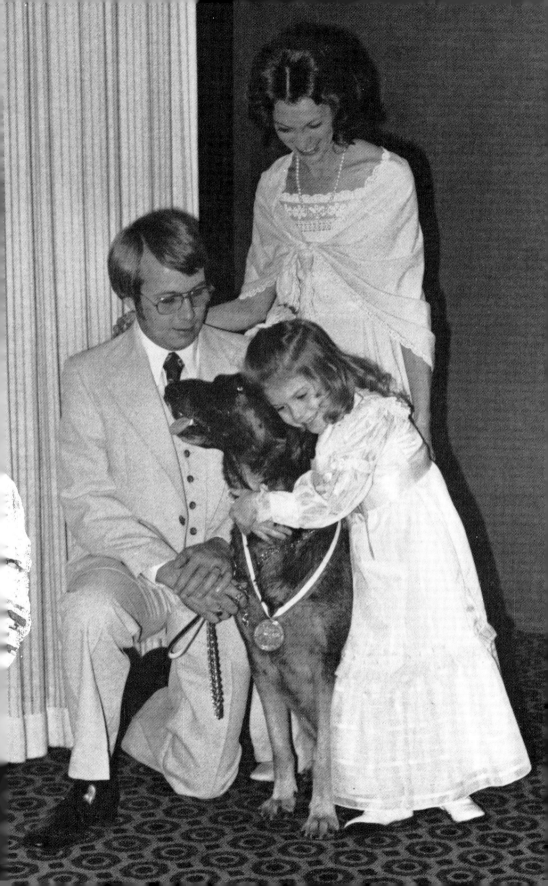

1978-Chessie poses with his family, the Hommes of Livingston, Montana. The Chesapeake Bay retriever struggled against a powerful current for almost fifteen minutes to save Kenny (r.) from a raging creek.

Although only a puppy, Rommel was able to rescue a two-year-old child. The exploit was worthy of a 2nd Place award.

Duke, a German shepherd, won a 3rd Place award by saving a young boy from a copperhead snake.

companies 1 killed, 60 wounded.

Present effective strength 245. Situation serious.

Place (not given) Oct. 3, 1918.

(signed) Whittlesey, Major
Released (n. given) Arrived (n. given)

308th

Band No. 316N16.

#7 Headquarters of C.O., 1st Bn., 308th Inf. to C.O., 308th Inf.

All quiet during the night. Our patrols indicate Germans withdrew during night. Sending further patrols now to verify this.

At 12:30 and 1:10 A.M. six shells from our own light artillery fell on us.

Many wounded here whom we cannot evacuate.

Need rations badly.

No word from D. or A. companies.

Place 294.7-276.3 Oct. 4, 1918
Released 7:20 A.M. Arrived 7:48 A.M.

(signed) Whittlesey, Major
308th Infantry

#8 Headquarters of C.O., 1st Bn., 308th Inf. to C.O., 308th Inf.

Germans are still around us tho in small numbers. We have been heavily shelled by mortars this morning. Present effective strength (A,B,C,E,H,G Cos) 175. K. Co. 307, 45, M. G. detachment 17; total here about 235.

Officers wounded: Lt. Harrington, A; Capt. Strohmel, C; Lt. Buehler, G; Lts. Peabody & Barenous, M. G.; Lt. Wilhelm, A, is missing.

Cover bad if we advance up the hill and very

difficult to move the wounded if we change position. Situation is cutting into our strength rapidly. Men are suffering from hunger and exposure; and the wounded are in very bad condition. Cannot support be sent at once?

Place 294.7-276.3 Oct. 4, 1918
Released 10:35 A.M. Arrived 10:58 A.M.
                    (signed) Whittlesey, Major 308th

#9 Headquarters of C.O., 1st Bn., 308th Inf. to C.O., 308th Inf.
     We are along the road parallel 276.4.
     Our own artillery is dropping a barrage directly on us.
     For Heaven's sake stop it!

Place (in msg) Oct. 4, 1918.
Released 3:00 P.M. Arrived 4:00 P.M.
                    (signed) Whittlesey,
                    Major, 308th Inf.

Now read that last fateful message once again. This was the message Cher Ami delivered and, in doing so, earned his right to hero status.

During World War II, one pigeon company delivered some 6,000 messages! This in a single month's time. The records are indeed impressive. Pigeons were often dropped from airplanes. The method consisted of placing the bird in a grocery bag with a slit in it and releasing the bag. When the bag had fallen to an altitude sensed by the bird as comfortable, it forced its way through the slit and winged its way homeward.

In Burma during World War II, most supplies were moved by large C-47 aircraft. Where they were unable to land, they delivered the supplies by dumping them out the cargo doors of the planes. The supplies floated down to the ground troops by parachute. These supply drops consisted of food, ammunition, clothing, medical supplies, the very necessities of war. The drops were not always made at the most convenient places. Once collected, the supplies had to be transported to the troops' location. Mules were used for this purpose.

You may have heard the term "mule skinner." Mules, as beasts of burden, are stubborn, and that's where "mule skinner" came from. The men who handled these mules used to have to beat them into motion, sometimes "beating the very skins off them." The mule skinners used a language that—to say the least—was colorful. Along any mountain or jungle trail, you could always tell where a mule was by the unceasing chorus of epithets offered by their handlers. "You lop-eared no-good son of a _____!"

Rosie was a typical army mule: long-eared, given to loud braying protests, and reluctant to do anything except eat and sleep. Ben, her handler, was a typical Burma GI. He perpetually needed a shave and a shower, looked like one of the characters out of a Bill Mauldin cartoon, and was about as rough and ready as he could be. His carbine was always slung over his shoulder, muzzle down so it could be whipped up to sling-firing position in a trice, should the occasion demand.

As the enemy retreated from the jungle, under the advance of the Allied troops, snipers were left behind in the trees with a supply of food and water. When both gave out, the sniper would open fire on whomever was about. Chances are that he would quickly be seen and killed, but not until he had worked havoc on the ground troops.

That's how Ben got hit.

He was working Rosie along a trail when there was the sharp crack of a rifle. Ben never knew what hit him. He slumped to the ground, unconscious, bleeding from the wound in his back. Rosie stopped in her tracks and looked down at her fallen handler. She brayed once or twice, and seeing no help coming, she bent over and grabbed Ben's carbine in her teeth. Using this and the sling that held it over the man's shoulder, Rosie backed along the trail, dragging Ben with her.

Ben embellishes the story as he tells it, and never tells it the same way twice. But apparently Rosie dragged Ben to safety, where he received help. Later, he rejoined the outfit, and when Rosie spotted him, she laid her ears back and brayed a greeting that warmed his heart. He rushed to her, threw his arms around her neck, and swore at her lovingly for five minutes without repeating a single word! As Ben later explained it, "That lop-eared S.O.B. wasn't trying to save my life. No, sir. She was trying to get that carbine in 'er teeth so she could take a shot at the Jap that got me."

Rodney was a horse. Now if Rodney had been a human, he'd have been a fat, strictly GI topkick, chewing on a cigar and knowing all the angles. Rodney was, in fact, a bay draft animal, part Thoroughbred and part Percheron.

General Summerall, writing about his own recollections of Rodney, described him thus:

"He was named after a distinguished Civil War officer, had a deep body, massive shoulders, powerful neck and legs, and the fine, intelligent head of that strain. From the Thoroughbred he inherited courage, endurance, large nostrils, and fine features. He stood 16 or 16½ hands high and weighed 1,600 pounds."

During the Spanish-American War, Rodney distinguished himself as a powerful wheel horse. In severe field conditions in Cuba, his unfailing courage under exhausting labor in heat and rough terrain earned him the admiration and affection of the men. He demonstrated his willingness, strength, and endurance by single-handedly hauling a gun into position when all his teammates were exhausted or wounded. Rodney was wounded in that engagement, though not disabled, and his popularity only increased.

At Chickamauga Park, Rodney served as a near-wheeler and never lost a day of service. At Fort Myer, Rodney was allowed to run loose, and for a while was used to haul hay into the stable lofts. But Rodney, being a typical soldier, soon learned that whenever a load of hay arrived, it meant work for him, and he would leave the stables at a gallop.

As age crept on, Rodney grew fat and became stiff from years of hard work. In time, instead of going out with the team, he was allowed to graze. Finally, he was officially retired by the War Department. When he died, he was buried with full military honors by the battery.

Following is a copy of an inscription appearing on the bronze memorial tablet commemorating the horses and mules that died during World War I, erected in the State, War and Navy Building by the American Red Star Animal Relief on October 21, 1921:

"This tablet commemorates the service and sufferings of the 243,135 horses and mules employed by the American Expeditionary Forces overseas during the great war which terminated November 11, 1918, and which resulted in the death of 68,682 of those animals. What they suffered is beyond words to describe. A fitting tribute to their important services has been given by the commander-in-chief of the American Expeditionary Forces, General John J. Pershing, who has written: 'The Army horses and mules proved of inestimable value in prosecuting the war to a successful conclusion. They were found in all the theaters of preparation and operation doing their silent but faithful work without the faculty of hoping for any reward or compensation.'"

Horse cavalry was last used in combat in the Mexican Border campaign and to a lesser degree during the early part of World War II in the Philippines.

Few know that horse troops rode again during the Saar campaign in Europe in 1944. The incident was dreamed up by an old advocate of retaining horses, Gen. George C. Patton.

In early November 1944, units of Patton's Third Army became stalled in the Saar-Moselle triangle. It had rained for days and the area was a quagmire; moreover, the weather prevented needed air support from getting airborne.

The Germans were holding well-fortified positions, adding to the dismay of the mechanized units advancing on the town of Dieuze. Orders came down to get on with the job

55

of clearing the enemy from the area.

Col. Charles (Hank) Reed, having some 60 German artillery horses, conceived an idea. He scrounged up saddles and other equipment and formed a troop of cavalry.

The horse unit operated more than a week, moving easily and silently through enemy fortifications, and rounded up hundreds of amazed Germans and captured several small towns.

Patton was so pleased with the accomplishment he sent detailed reports of the unique operation to Allied headquarters. He maintained that one horse cavalry division in the African and Sicily campaigns would have been equal to a whole corps of mechanized cavalry.

On Saturday, 15 December 1956, on high plains of Fort Carson, Colorado, a colorful era passed into history. The occasion was the deactivation of the 35th Quartermaster Company (Pack). A very stirring ceremony took place on the Fort Carson Drill Field. Men and animals with pack equipment were lined up on the field in normal review formation. The adjutant read the deactivation order. He was followed in turn by Maj. Gen. Harry P. Storke, Commanding General, Headquarters Fort Carson and Headquarters 9th Infantry Division. General Storke gave a very stirring talk, extolling the role of the army mule in the many campaigns in which he was used by the United States Army.

Men and animals passed in review for the last time. It was a sad occasion for many old timers, who had given many long years of service with the animal units. As part of the review was an old animal-drawn buckboard, carrying several of the old-time sergeants. In an extension to the reviewing stand were army mule Trotter of the 35th QM Co. (Pk), and army mule Hambone of A Btry 4th FA Bn (Pk), who took part in receiving the review.

Upon completion of the review, enlisted men mounted on horses brought the colors and guidons before the commanding general, and with due ceremony, these guidons and colors were lowered and cased, symbolizing the deactivation of these units. Upon retirement of the colors and guidons army mules Trotter and Hambone were brought before the commanding general and each was given a citation. The citation of army mule Trotter is quoted as follows:

Certificate of Recognition: Trotter

In recognition of outstanding service given during the period of 6 June 1949 to 15 December 1956 with the 35th Quartermaster Pack Company, this certificate is awarded to United States Army Mule 583R, also known as Trotter.

Your long and devoted service has included two round-trip overland tours of the 190-mile distance to Cheyenne, Wyoming, and four round-trip tours to Camp Hale, 150 miles distant, as well as participation in all exercises conducted at Camp Hale since 1949. Special recognition is also made of your exceptional abilities in that you are the single one out of thousands who is master of four gaits: the walk, trot, gallop, and pace.

The presentation of this certificate on the occasion of the deactivation of Army mules is accompanied by the firm hope that your retirement will not be plagued with those horrors which, in times past, have caused you to unburden yourself rather hurriedly of riders and other equipment—a glimpse of either of those hideous devices, the umbrella or the bicycle.

Presented at Fort Carson, Colorado, this 15th day of December, 1956.

H. P. STORKE
Major General, USA
Commanding

Certificate of Recognition: Hambone

In recognition of outstanding service during the period of 4 January 1943 to 15 December 1956 with the United States Army, and more specifically, from May 1948 to the present with A Battery, 4th Field Artillery Battalion (Pack), this certificate is awarded to United States Army Mule 9Y11, known affectionately to his public as Hambone.

57

Your long, devoted and well-publicized service has included maneuvers during three winters at Camp Hale and two round trips to Cheyenne, Wyoming, the last of which was made entirely overland during the summer of 1956.

Special commendation is due to you for your extraordinary abilities displayed in jumping events, and for the record of having never lost a mule jumping contest, as well as for your phenomenal success in bettering all except the first place winner in a competition with horses at Fort Carson in 1950.

In addition, your exhibition jumping at the International Stock Show in Chicago in 1950, at the Pikes Peak Rodeo in 1954, and at other equestrian functions has been a credit both to yourself and the United States Army.

In view of these outstanding achievements, your refusals to perform such menial tasks as carrying a pack and your refraining from associating with other mules are hereby recognized as privileges specifically accorded to you.

Presented at Fort Carson, Colorado, this 15th day of December, 1956.

H. P. STORKE
Major General, USA
Commanding

Upon completion of the citations both army mules were returned to their position in the reviewing stand. Thereupon an army helicopter which had been hovering in the background flew in front of the receiving stand and gave salute to the two mules by dipping its fuselage; thus paying homage to the army mule and accepting the responsibility of carrying on their mission.

Had we been setting out to prove a point, there would, at this time, be no question that animals have contributed in heroic fashion to all of man's war efforts.

Animals aren't able to understand the principles that drive men to make war on one another. It is not patriotism, freedom, or any other rallying cries that impel animals to acts of heroism in combat. No, what makes an animal heroic in wartime is the same force that leads to heroism in time of peace. It is love for mankind. An animal's love is selfless and subordinates the animal to the needs of the human he serves or lives with.

Man rewards the animal hero with the same baubles with which he rewards himself. He pins his own medals on the beast, increases his unofficial rank, and provides him with suitable press coverage, announcing to all and sundry that the animal is indeed a hero. While these are the rewards that men may strive for, they are meaningless to the animal.

But at all of these ceremonies, there is always at least one soldier who will, almost as an afterthought, pat the animal on the head, scratch behind an ear, and whisper the words, "Good boy!"

To the animal, that is the ultimate accolade.

CHAPTER THREE

DOG OF THE YEAR

Each year for twenty-four years, a panel of three highly respected judges has selected the dog that has performed the most outstanding act of courage leading to the saving of life or property. Sponsored by Ken-L Ration dog food, a division of The Quaker Oats Company, the Dog Hero of the Year Award has become a tradition honoring canine bravery.

The yearly Dog Hero and his owners receive the Ken-L Ration Gold Medal, a $1,000 U.S. savings bond, a year's supply of dog food, and a gold-plated leash and collar. More than this, the winner receives the recognition he or she deserves.

The extraordinary Dog Heroes over the years have been credited with saving the lives of nearly 225 humans and 300 animals.

Chicago, 1954, was the location of the inaugural Dog Hero fete. The winner, Tang, a large collie, had saved the lives of five children by leaping four times in front of automobiles to push the children out of their paths. On another occasion, Tang planted himself in front of a truck, howling and barking, until the driver discovered a two-year-old stowaway, who—had she not been found—would have fallen to the pavement the moment the truck began to move.

Although Tang's courage was magnificent, through the years his feats have been equaled or exceeded by countless dogs nationwide who, displaying incredible tenacity, bravery, and loyalty, have distinguished themselves in a variety of ways, lending credence to the well-deserved title of "man's best friend."

GRIZZLY BEAR

Grizzly Bear, an extremely gentle St. Bernard from Denali, Alaska, battled and finally routed a real grizzly bear that had attacked and mauled his mistress.

The 180-pound, twenty-month-old dog, amazingly enough, had always been called "Grizzly Bear" rather than by his long, officially registered name of Polar Blu Samaritan von Barri. He is owned by Mr. and Mrs. David Gratias of Denali, who own and operate a lodge and live in a cabin behind the main building.

Around noon one cold spring day, Mrs. Gratias heard a noise in the backyard. Since her husband was working elsewhere at the time, she went to investigate. She went out the front door, the only entrance to the cabin, leaving it open with her two-year-old daughter, Theresa, sleeping just inside. She also unleashed Grizzly Bear, so he could run around while she was outside. But as she reached the backyard, she discovered a young grizzly bear cub. Assuming that its mother must be near, she raced back toward the open front door. As she rounded the corner of the house, she came face to face with the mother grizzly.

The huge beast raised itself up to its eight-foot height and grabbed at her. Mrs. Gratias, conscious only of the fact that she must get to the open door and protect her daughter, attempted to sidestep the animal. But her feet slipped on the icy ground. She fell, and lay stunned by the force of her fall.

In a flash, the grizzly was upon her, raking her cheek

with one paw while it sank the other deep into her shoulder. But as it bent down to inflict a possibly fatal bite, the bear was suddenly staggered backwards as Grizzly Bear crashed into it with every ounce of his 180 pounds. Roaring with rage, the bear came back at Mrs. Gratias, but the dog, maneuvering smartly and slashing at the bear with his teeth and paws, managed to keep himself constantly between the animal and his helpless mistress.

At this moment, Mrs. Gratias, overcome with terror and weakened by loss of blood, lapsed into unconsciousness. When she came to, the dog was licking her face in an attempt to revive her. Sitting up dazedly, she suddenly remembered what had happened. She raced to the open door, to find Theresa inside, sleeping soundly. The bear had vanished.

Mrs. Gratias's wounds eventually healed, and, fortunately, the claw marks on her face were not so deep as to cause disfiguration. Although Grizzly Bear was spotted with blood, no wounds were found, and it was assumed that the blood had come from either Mrs. Gratias or the bear itself. But the memory of the horrible experience caused Mrs. Gratias to travel to Anchorage, 350 miles away, and stay with relatives until the terror of the incident had passed.

TANG

Winner of the first annual Ken-L Ration gold medal award as America's Dog Hero of the Year was Tang, a huge, friendly collie from Denison, Texas. Owned by Air Force Captain and Mrs. Maurice Dyer, this dog, possessing a protective instinct to a remarkable degree, saved no fewer than five children from death or severe injury.

Four times he leaped in front of swift-moving automobiles and thrust his powerful bulk against a child to push the tot to the curb just split seconds before tragedy could strike. On another occasion, he planted himself squarely in front of a parked milk delivery truck and refused to budge, barking loudly all the while. When the puzzled driver alighted to ascertain the cause of the strange behavior of the normally friendly dog, he found that a two-year-old girl had clambered into the back of his truck, from which she would almost certainly have fallen. The moment she was removed, Tang ceased his barking and returned placidly to the sidewalk.

Tang's story is a heartwarming one. The Dyers had lost their own collie, and, in their grief, could not bring themselves to adopt another. But a veterinarian finally persuaded them to "just look" at Tang, who, little more than a puppy, had been the victim of mistreatment and was completely mistrustful of humans, especially children. "Something in his eyes" reminded the Dyers of their own lost dog, and with numerous misgivings, they took him home.

Affection and kindly care worked wonders with Tang, and in six months he had developed into a powerful but friendly dog, who without any training whatsoever had established himself as the protector of children at the air base in Alaska at which Captain Dyer was stationed. As speeding army trucks rumbled past the homes of the military personnel, Tang would herd his charges back from the road, and twice he actually pushed tiny tots from directly in front of the automobiles.

Transferred to Perrin Air Force Base, Captain Dyer took up residence in nearby Denison, Texas. There, the Dyers and their neighbors were witnesses to the sight of Tang saving two more children in similar fashion.

Self-appointed nursemaid and baby-sitter for the whole neighborhood, Tang became a real celebrity in Denison. And when the news came that he had been unanimously selected as the winner of the first national award for dog heroes, the children of the neighborhood organized an impromptu parade for him.

This greathearted dog passed away in 1958, but the children he loved did not forget him. He was laid away in a peaceful glen, and around his grave the children play to this day. Tang would have wished it no other way.

TAFFY

An appealing honey-colored cocker spaniel from Coeur d'Alene, Idaho, named Taffy, owned by Mr. and Mrs. Ken Wilson of that city, was instrumental in saving her little master, Stevie Wilson, three, from a watery grave at the bottom of icy Fernan Lake.

Taffy's exploit began when Stevie's father, wishing to try out a saddle horse, went to a corral at the edge of the lake. Stevie and Taffy were placed in a spot from which they could not get into trouble. One of the neighbors, however, let the child and dog out, and the two proceeded to roam about.

Wilson, riding the horse about the corral, was surprised to see Taffy suddenly come bounding into the enclosure, barking excitedly and racing about the horse. Although puzzled by the dog's unusual actions, Wilson at first did not pay particular attention, thinking that the boy was in a place where he was safe from harm.

Taffy, realizing that her antics were not succeeding in getting Wilson to understand, suddenly broke away and dashed toward the lake. A moment or two later, she reappeared, dripping wet, barking at the top of her lungs, and nipping at the horse's legs until Wilson was almost thrown from his mount.

Suddenly realizing that the dog would never leap into the cold lake water unless something was amiss, Wilson stopped and shouted to the neighbor to ask if Stevie was safe. When the neighbor replied that he had let the child out, Wilson leaped off the horse and set out after the racing Taffy. The excited dog led him to the lake edge, where he saw Stevie's bright red mackinaw floating on the surface.

Jumping into the four-foot-deep water, Wilson lifted his unconscious son from the bottom of the clear lake. While neighbors summoned a pulmotor, he worked over the tot with artificial respiration. For six hours, after being taken to the Wilson home, the youngster hovered between life and death.

Just before midnight, his eyelids flickered open for the

first time, and the first thing that met his eyes was Taffy, crouched in a prayerful attitude beside his bed.

An attending physician, shaking his head in wonderment at the child's return to the land of the living, said that undoubtedly just a few more moments at the bottom of the icy lake would have proved fatal.

LASSIE

Because his dog was deliberately disobedient, Gary Gustafson, six, of San Carlos, California, is alive today. The deed that prevented a tragedy was responsible for the selection of his dog, Lassie, a Shetland Sheepdog, as Dog Hero of the Year in 1956.

Young Gary, unhappy because a donkey bought for him proved to be too large, was offered his choice of a litter of Shetland Sheepdogs. The one that caught his fancy was small and rather sickly, but Gary liked her and insisted on choosing her over the more healthy-looking of the lot. It was a decision that was to save his life.

Gary's parents, Mr. and Mrs. Clayton Gustafson, gave the dog an obedience training course, an activity in which Lassie displayed remarkable intelligence. She became Gary's virtual shadow, and followed him about everywhere. At night, she would settle herself near his door and never budge from that spot until the morning.

Around midnight one night, the elder Gustafsons were roused from deep slumber by Lassie, who rushed into their bedroom, barking and whining, and even pulling at their bedclothes. Astounded by the dog's strange actions, for she had been taught never to enter their room, they at first attempted to order her back to Gary's room at the other end of the house.

Lassie stubbornly refused to leave, and even increased her whining and barking and pulling at their bedclothes. They finally decided that she must want to go outside. But when Mr. Gustafson took her to the door, she retreated, and began racing back and forth between the door and Gary's room, indicating that she wished to be followed. With a sigh of resignation, Mr. Gustafson followed her into Gary's bedroom, there to find Gary lying on the floor in a pool of blood, having suffered a hemorrhage as the aftermath of a tonsillectomy the previous week.

Rushed to a hospital, Gary was given emergency treatment, and physicians there said that another fifteen minutes' delay would have cost the youngster his life. Lassie, the puppy that Gary insisted on choosing, had proven herself the prize of the litter.

BLAZE

A beautiful white-faced collie named Blaze became the second of his breed to become Dog Hero of the Year and earn the gold medal for his owners, Mr. and Mrs. Duane Hecox of Timewell, Illinois.

A neighbor, forced to leave home for several days on personal business, had left Blaze's mother with the Hecoxes, and the arrival of puppies came as quite a surprise. As a reward for taking care of the mother and the pups, the owner gave them the biggest and handsomest of the lot, Blaze.

One day, while little Dawn Hecox, two and a half, was playing in the yard on the Hecox farm, the child decided to get a better look at some baby pigs which were in a fenced-in enclosure nearby. She crawled through the fence, infuriating the mother sow, who charged her, knocked her to the ground, and was severely mauling and biting the child when Blaze, a short distance away, went into action.

Despite an ever-present fear he had of this massive hog, Blaze never hesitated. With a single bound, he cleared the fence and attacked the sow so savagely that she gave ground. The badly injured child, shocked and bleeding, was given enough time to crawl back through the fence to safety.

Hearing the commotion, the parents rushed to the scene, picked up their stunned and bleeding child, and hurried her to the hospital. There it was found that four teeth had been knocked out, numerous severe bites had been sustained, and she was in a state of shock. For two days, she was on the critical list, and was under the constant care of physicians for three weeks before recovering.

DUTCHESS

The 1958 gold medal was captured by Dutchess, a German shepherd, owned by Mr. and Mrs. Donald Phillippi of Excelsior, Minnesota. Dutchess saved Linda Phillippi from death by drowning, in an almost unbelievable feat of courage and stamina.

The performance that won for her the highest accolade of the year began on a pleasant afternoon, when Mr. Phillippi took three of his children for a ride on Lake William in his homemade hydroplane. The dog watched idly from the shore, since the lake adjoins the Phillippi property.

Suddenly, as they neared the middle of the lake, the boat capsized while making a turn, and all occupants were thrown into the deep water. Mr. Phillippi was in a real quandary, for, in addition to himself, only one of the group, Johnny, eleven, could swim. The other children, Matthew, six, and Linda, ten, hung on desperately to the side of the overturned craft, with their father striving to keep their heads above water. The younger children were on the verge of panic, and were fast losing their grip on the boat.

Dutchess, 150 yards away on shore, sensed immediately what had happened. Without an instant's hesitation, she leaped into the water and ate up the distance to the scene with powerful strokes. As she reached the boat, Mr. Phillippi made a sudden and daring decision, for the boat was sinking rapidly and catastrophe was staring him in the face. He ordered Linda to grasp Dutchess's collar. As she did so, the dog, without a word of command, turned abruptly and struck out for shore, towing the almost dead weight of the girl behind her.

As Dutchess stumbled ashore after finishing the 150-yard swim, Linda collapsed exhausted on the bank. Dutchess now turned and was about to strike out for the boat again, when she saw that a neighbor had reached the scene in his own boat and was taking the other survivors to safety.

LADY

The first mongrel, or mixed breed, ever to capture the gold medal was the 1959 winner, Lady, a collie-shepherd. Lady's owners were Mr. and Mrs. Walter Abel of Mehlville, Missouri, whose son Tommy is alive today only because of the intelligence and persistence of this "curbstone setter."

It was a dark, cold February afternoon when little Tommy, then three years old, wandered away from his suburban home near St. Louis. As he roamed about, accompanied by Lady, the tyke failed to realize that he was getting farther and farther away from familiar territory. As dusk approached and the afternoon grew chill, the child suddenly found himself mired in the mud of a swamp, far from any human habitation.

A search party, organized after the parents discovered his absence, had given up after failing to come anywhere near the place where Tommy was caught. The child, hysterical and exhausted, was so spent that he could no longer even cry for help. At this point, Lady, who had been watching his unsuccessful efforts to free himself, hurried away. But this was no abandonment of her little master.

Racing through the desolate woods and barking at the top of her lungs, Lady happened upon two telephone linemen who were in the vicinity repairing a break in the lines. The unusual actions of the dog—for Lady was rushing back and forth and whining—indicated that she wished them to follow her. Finally convinced that something was wrong, they shouldered their equipment and followed her.

After traveling so far that they decided they would abandon the whole idea after climbing the next hill, they reached the crest of the hill and found below them the exhausted child, too worn out to utter a sound, up to his knees in the sticky mud as darkness was closing about him.

69

With great difficulty, they succeeded in freeing him and brought him home to his despairing parents.

KEG

The second German shepherd to reign as National Dog Hero of the Year was the 1960 winner, Keg, owned by Mr. and Mrs. William McMannis of Bozeman, Montana.

Mr. McMannis, a professor of geology at Montana State College, had left for the school one morning, and Mrs. McMannis, who was doing some shopping, had left little Karen, their eighteen-month-old daughter, in the care of a neighbor.

Playing with her inseparable companion, Keg, the child wandered to the edge of the backyard, then suddenly decided that she would cross a footbridge that spanned Kelly Creek, normally a quiet little stream but at this time at flood stage. As she toddled along the bridge, she suddenly lost her balance and fell backward into the torrent.

Struck dumb with horror and fear, the neighbor saw the huge Keg, an immensely powerful dog, leap into the angry waters after the child. As he reached her side, he attempted to seize her dress, but could not manage to get a secure grip. Unable to hold her otherwise, he clamped his teeth into her shoulder blade, and with powerful strokes, began moving steadily toward the shore as they were swept downstream.

Battling the current with a furious determination, he managed to reach a spot where the stream widened, and pulled the unconscious child part way up the bank to where the pursuing neighbor could reach them. Rushed to a Bozeman hospital, the child was given oxygen for two hours, and four hours later was pronounced out of danger.

DUKE

Fire, perhaps the most dreaded of all dangers to a dog, was responsible for the near-tragedy that won for Duke, a rollicking collie from Niles, Ohio, the gold medal as Dog Hero of 1961.

It was a blustery March afternoon when little Penny Grantz, ten, daughter of Mr. and Mrs. John Grantz of Niles, went to the backyard to burn some papers. The capricious wind caused the child's skirt to billow and suddenly burst into flames as flying ashes caught it. The terrified girl, panic-stricken, began to race toward the house, twenty-five yards away.

Duke, playing nearby, took in the situation with a glance. Barking loudly, he overtook the child and, although possessing the average animal's dread of fire, seized her flaming skirt in his teeth and tore and pawed the garment off her to the ground, sustaining burns to his mouth in the process.

Penny's father, a night worker who was asleep at the time, heard the commotion and dashed from the house. By this time the flames had spread to her blouse and other clothing, and he ripped these off and rushed her to a hospital. There she remained for nine weeks, and physicians attending her said that had it not been for Duke's heroic action, she would probably have died.

BEGGAR

One of the largest dogs ever to become Dog Hero of the Year was a 165-pound female St. Bernard named Beggar, owned by Mr. and Mrs. Robert D. Mitchell of Sacramento, California.

Beggar's heroic action followed the disappearance of her little master, Bobby Mitchell, three, from the lad's home in Carmichael, California, where the family resided at the time. By the time that his mother, busy with housework, discovered his absence, Bobby had wandered far from home and was hopelessly lost. A search party organized by police and sheriffs failed to find any trace of him.

A Boy Scout troop encamped along the rain-swollen American River came across the child and Beggar, both soaking wet, a few feet from the river's edge and more than a mile from their home. Leading the shivering child by the sleeve, and with her protective instincts fully aroused, the massive dog at first refused to surrender her little charge to the Scouts.

When a family friend was brought to the scene, however, she gave him up docilely and trotted home after them. There the child's wet clothing was removed, and tooth marks on his body confirmed his story of how he had fallen into the river and Beggar had seized him in her huge jaws and swum to the bank.

DUTCH

A fun-loving German shepherd from Troy, Pennsylvania, who leaped into twelve-foot-deep water to rescue a four-year-old boy and thereby save the life of his three-year-old brother as well, was declared winner of the tenth annual gold medal in 1963 as America's Dog Hero of the Year.

Dutch, a friendly, bouncy canine who was bought for twenty-five dollars as a pup and became one of the greatest bargains in history, leaped from the obscurity of a small Pennsylvania town to nationwide fame when he was instrumental in saving the lives of two small boys.

On this occasion, Hugh Hawthorne, four, and his little brother, Gordon, three, were playing on a pier which extends into the water of a pond near their home on the outskirts of Troy. Both children had been forbidden to approach this area, but like many children of their age, they "just forgot."

As they scuffled on the pier, Gordon suddenly lost his balance and tumbled into the water. Horror-stricken, Hugh plunged in to save him. Neither child could swim a stroke.

Taking in the situation at a glance, Dutch, who had been looking on, raced onto the pier and leaped into the water, then standing at a cold thirty-four degrees. With powerful strokes, he made his way to Hugh and grabbed the lad by the ankle. Paddling swiftly, he towed the spluttering lad to shore. Gordon, floating face downward, still remained in the water.

The clamor set up by Dutch and Hugh brought the boys' mother, Mrs. Gerald Hawthorne, to the scene on the run. Although nearly nine months pregnant, she dived into the water, and being a good swimmer, was able to tow her unconscious son to shore.

Having watched a demonstration of mouth-to-mouth resuscitation on a television station five months before, she began efforts to revive Gordon, who was "blue in the face, almost rigid, and with eyes open as though dead." Long minutes later, he gave a gurgle, and she rushed to the telephone and summoned aid.

A policeman arriving on the scene shortly afterward helped with the mouth-to-mouth resuscitation efforts, and a doctor then put his respiratory machine to work. Although apparently "dead" three times, the lad was finally revived at Troy Memorial Hospital and was allowed to return home at noon the next day. Dutch's heroic rescue had saved the life of not just one lad, but two.

BUDDY

A camera-shy collie from Budd Lake, New Jersey, who saved nearly three hundred goats in a raging fire that leveled most of his master's goat dairy farm, was named winner of the gold medal in 1964.

Buddy, a twenty-month-old purebred, was lauded by businessmen throughout the nation after his courageous feat one cold January morning and rightfully earned the additional title of "businessman's best friend."

In the early hours of the morning, a fire had been roaring in the farm's maternity barn for some time before Buddy's frantic barks of warning were heard by his masters, Mr. and Mrs. Matthew S. Crinkley, Jr. Investigating the commotion, the Crinkleys rushed to the window only to see the walls and roof of the barn tumbling into a flaming pile of ruin.

Racing to the yard, they were astonished and elated to see Buddy marching back and forth with the efficiency of a Prussian general, watching over the entire flock of seventy expectant goats he had herded out of the barn. Despite severe burns on his paws and nasal damage from smoke inhalation, Buddy had maneuvered to safety an entire herd of animals that are notoriously stubborn, by pushing them and nipping at their feet.

The warning of this dedicated farm dog allowed the Crinkleys just enough time to save a second barn, which housed their remaining thirty goats, by wetting down a roof where sparks were beginning to ignite the structure. The hundred goats, together with those since born of the expectant mothers, later constituted a flock of nearly three hundred goats that would surely have been lost had it not been for this intelligent and devoted collie.

The Crinkleys' goat dairy, one of the nation's largest, provides a vitally important service to thousands of people living in the northeastern states. Goat's milk is a valuable nutriment for various types of physical illnesses, including ulcers and other digestive disorders. The loss of this herd would have created hardship, especially for children, as few other large goat dairies exist in that part of the nation.

HERO

A pooch named Hero was named America's Dog Hero of the Year after saving the life of a small boy. Hero, a young Blue Merle collie, had been in the show ring briefly, but he much preferred driving cattle. His owner, Mrs. George Jolley of Priest River, Idaho, although convinced that Hero had a bright future as a show dog, reluctantly put her dreams away and allowed him to do the thing he loved best, cutting and driving the farm animals, a job at which he excelled.

One day, while she was in the barn loft pitching hay down to the horses that Hero was herding in from the pasture, her two-and-one-half year-old son, Shawn, was playing beside her. She didn't realize he had disappeared until she heard him scream, and she looked down to see the little fellow racing across the barn floor, with a maddened horse thundering after him.

Mrs. Jolley screamed for Hero, even though she had no idea where he was at the moment. Meanwhile, Shawn, running as fast as his little legs would carry him, reached the end of the barn and attempted to slide to safety under a tractor parked there. But, tragically, his denim jacket caught on a projecting piece of the vehicle, and he found himself hopelessly trapped, unable to move in any direction. He could only scream in terror as the horse raised its feet to stamp out his life.

At this horrible moment, a blue-gray form came hurtling through the air. It was Hero. Leaping up at the horse, he seized it by the nostrils and hung on grimly. Snorting with rage and pain, the horse swung the dog from side to side and finally hurled him viciously against the tractor, where he crumpled in a heap.

Amazingly, he was up the next instant and flying back at the animal, using teeth and claws and adamantly refusing to retreat. Stationing himself between the raging animal and the child, he battled the horse until Mrs. Jolley managed to reach the child, release him from the tractor's projecting edge, and pull him under the vehicle with her.

But in the meantime, Hero had been taking a fearful beating. Several times the horse's lashing hooves had caught him squarely in the mouth, and the huge animal's feet were making a bloody mess of the dog's forepaws. But the indomitable dog steadfastly refused to take a backward step.

By this time, however, Mrs. Jolley had managed to seize a stick, and she began jabbing at the animal as Hero fought it tooth and nail. Suddenly, the horse broke off the fight and rushed out the far door, with Hero in pursuit. Only when he saw the animal disappear into the farthest end of the pasture did the gallant dog sink to the ground with blood pouring from its mouth.

More dead than alive, Hero was rushed to a veterinarian in Spokane, forty-five miles away. There, it was found that he had suffered severe internal injuries, five ribs had been broken, and four teeth had been knocked out. But it was typical of this greathearted dog that five weeks later he was back in the show ring, earning points toward the coveted rank of "champion."

Who could deny that he had already earned that title!

PATCHES

One of the most incredible rescues in all canine history earned for a Spanaway, Washington, mongrel the gold medal as America's Dog Hero of the Year for 1965.

He was Patches, a collie-malamute, and only the second mixed-breed in the history of the award to capture the top spot.

The amazing exploit, or series of exploits, that earned for Patches the gold medal took place on a cold December night at Lake Spanaway, just south of Tacoma. Patches' owner, Marvin Scott, owner of a furniture store, returned home from work about 10 P.M. The thermometer was hovering around zero, and Scott informed his wife that he was going down to a small pier below their lake home to check on possible ice damage to a patrol boat moored there. Patches "tagged along," a circumstance for which Scott would ever after be thankful.

Noting that a film of ice was beginning to form around the boat, Scott attempted to push on the stern line with a piece of timber. But he did not realize that spray from the lake had made the pier boards glassy with ice, and as he pushed with the timber he slipped from the pier, his body struck a floating dock causing him to tear virtually all of the tendons and muscles in both legs, and he rolled off into the icy, fifteen-foot-deep water and went under.

Suddenly, while still below the surface, he felt something grasp him by the hair. It was Patches, who had leaped into the icy waters and was holding him firmly. Patches pulled the dazed and shivering man to the surface, then towed him nearly twenty feet to where he could seize the edge of the floating dock. Dimly aware that the dog, too, was by now nearly drowning and was almost exhausted from his rescue efforts, Scott managed to push him onto the dock.

But as Scott, his legs immobile and useless, vainly attempted to climb onto the dock himself, the combination of the frigid water, his terrible injuries, and the water he had swallowed caused him to black out and his grip on the dock loosened. He fell back into the water and went under.

But again it was Patches to the rescue. The courageous dog leaped in instantly, seized him by the hair, and this time pulled him about four feet to the dock. After Scott had recovered enough to push Patches onto the dock, the man hung on grimly and screamed for help, but with the late hour and the wind against him, his cries could not be heard. At this critical moment, when Scott was certain each moment would be his last, Patches once more proved to be the difference between life and death.

Bracing his four feet firmly on the dock boards, Patches grasped Scott's overcoat collar and tugged with might and main. Encouraged by this unexpected assistance, Scott struggled with every ounce of strength he had left, and somehow, between the two of them, the gasping man was able to pull his body up onto the dock.

After he had regained his breath, Scott began crawling toward the house, with Patches in front of him holding tenaciously to his collar and using every bit of strength he possessed to help pull the shivering and agonized man along. The two laboriously made their way in this fashion up a rock-studded, three-hundred-foot slope to a point near the back door, where Scott was able to throw a stone against the door and alert his wife.

Taken to Tacoma General Hospital, Scott hovered between life and death for twenty-five days, with pneumonia a constant threat in addition to the massive operations required on both of his legs. It was June 14 of the following year before he was able to return to work, using two canes to get about.

MIJO

An immensely powerful, 180-pound St. Bernard named Mijo, from Anchorage, Alaska, was named Dog Hero of the Year for 1967.

The first canine from the forty-ninth state ever to triumph in this national competition, Mijo saved the life of her thirteen-year-old mistress, Philiciann Bennett.

The amazing exploit of Mijo, owned by Mr. and Mrs. Jake Bennett of Anchorage, began on a September day when, just after dinner, Philiciann and Mitchell asked permission of their parents to take the dog for a walk. Freed of her leash but wearing a neck chain, Mijo was romping on the edge of a water-filled gravel pit with the children when suddenly the ground, softened by rain, slid beneath them. Philiciann found herself in water up to her neck, with Mitchell some distance away but safely high and dry for the moment.

A competent swimmer, the girl attempted to "push off," but to her horror discovered that the effort only made her sink deeper into the quicksandlike gravel. At this point, realizing that she could not free her feet, and with the water now up to her chin, the panic-stricken girl screamed for help. Mitchell began to scramble down the steep embankment to reach her side, totally unaware that a similar fate might befall him.

At this terrible moment of crisis, the girl saw Mijo making her way toward her. After circling apparently aimlessly in front of Philiciann, the dog suddenly lowered her head and came up directly beneath her. As a drowning man would clutch at a straw, the girl made a desperate grab for the dog's chain collar and hung on grimly.

With the first of her powerful strokes, Mijo yanked the girl's feet free of the clinging mud and headed for open water. Once away from the treacherous mud, the dog turned and, towing the 105-pound girl along, swam to a nearby bank and pulled her partway up the bank to safety. Mitchell, watching the scene in amazement, now managed to make his way safely out of danger also.

RINGO

Mrs. Raymond Saleh, mother of four children, was busy with her household work in Euless, Texas, just before Christmas in 1965. She looked up from her chores to see a nondescript puppy pawing at the back door. Mrs. Saleh, who had been secretly preparing to purchase a Basset hound for the children at the Yuletide season, shouted and waved her arms at the puppy, who became frightened and hurried away.

But a few minutes later, when Mrs. Saleh chanced to go to the garage for something, she found the forlorn little thing attempting, in his hunger, to eat a mop. The softhearted woman, unable to stand the sight, picked up the pitiful little creature and brought him into the house, where it became evident that he had not eaten for a long time. She gave him his fill to eat, whereupon he curled up on the rug and went to sleep. When the children came home and saw the furry little thing on the rug, they decided quickly that "this was their dog," and they would have no other. With a sigh of resignation, the Salehs gave in and said the newcomer could stay.

Taken to the veterinarian for shots, the dog was regarded with considerable curiosity. It was finally decided that he could safely be termed a "part St. Bernard." The other part, which some observers guessed might be Chow, was a mystery. But the Salehs didn't care, and the children didn't care. The dog was theirs, and that's all that mattered. Because of his great white mane, and because the Beatles were popular at the time, they decided to call him "Ringo."

Ringo's great exploit began on a day when his little master, two-and-one-half-year-old Randy Saleh, wandered away from home just fifteen minutes before a gate was to be installed to stop the child's constant roaming. A two-hour police search failed to locate the child.

79

But about this time, Harley Jones, a school maintenance employee, driving along busy and dangerous Pipeline Road three quarters of a mile from the Saleh home, found himself halted by a long line of cars ahead of him as he crossed a hill and approached a blind curve. Motorists in the line of forty cars warned Jones that there was a "mad dog in the road ahead." He parked his car and went to the head of the line to investigate.

As he walked around the curve, he saw Ringo, resolutely stationed in the center of the road, blocking cars and even leaping against their fenders to halt the vehicles. Just a few feet ahead, and unseen, was little Randy, playing in the center of the heavily traveled roadway, as he had been doing for nearly fifteen minutes.

Jones looked on in wonder as the dog, after stopping a car, would rush back to the child and nudge him to the side of the roadway. But the little fellow, apparently thinking it was some sort of game, would immediately scurry back to the center of the highway and sit there, laughing. The dog, almost exhausted from nearly a quarter of an hour of this, was almost frantic, but he continued to race toward every oncoming car to halt it before his little charge could be hit.

Approaching cautiously because of the dog's highly aroused protective instinct, Jones talked soothingly to Ringo, and finally calmed him enough to permit the man to pick up the child. With Ringo's teeth menacingly at the calf of his leg every step of the way, Jones managed to gain the side of the road. The dog now relaxed, and allowed the automobiles to pass without incident.

TOP

A courageous child-loving Great Dane named Top, from Los Angeles, California, who saved two children from death or severe injury by two heroic deeds within eight weeks, was the winner of the gold medal in 1969.

Owned by a young German immigrant actor, Axel Patzwaldt, twenty-five, the harlequin-type dog will always limp noticeably on his right rear leg, which was shattered when he was struck by a truck as he pushed a young girl from the path of the swift-moving vehicle. But the injury failed to prevent Top from initiating the rescue of a two-year-old child from drowning just eight weeks later.

The huge dog's exploits began on an April day when an eleven-year-old neighbor girl was allowed to take him for a walk. A short distance from home, she started across the street, not noticing that a large truck was swiftly approaching. Suddenly realizing that the child was unaware of her danger, Top barked loudly, jumped in front of her, and pushed her backward, out of the way. She was unhurt, but Top was not so lucky. The truck hit him, breaking his right rear leg.

He was rushed to an animal hospital, where the leg was set and placed in a cast. His master took him home, and for seven weeks Top limped about painfully. Then, one week after the cast was removed, Patzwaldt let him out into the apartment house backyard, which contained a swimming pool. Just a few seconds later, Top came bounding back to the door, soaking wet and barking at the top of his lungs.

Patzwaldt and other residents ran to find out the reason for his noisemaking. They followed the excited and wildly-barking dog to the pool, and looked down to see the apparently lifeless body of two-year-old Christopher Conley, of the same address, lying on the bottom in six feet of water. Obviously, Top had leaped into the pool in an attempt to aid the child, and failing in that, had summoned help by his loud and continual barking.

A former lifeguard, Patzwaldt dove into the pool and brought the child out. Although the boy was apparently dead, the man began mouth-to-mouth resuscitation efforts while others called a fire rescue squad. By the time the firemen arrived, Patzwaldt had managed to arouse a spark of life in the youngster. Rushed to Citizens Emergency Hospital in West Hollywood, the child began to show signs of improvement, and eight hours later was pronounced out of danger.

The first Great Dane ever to gain this honor, the young dog later was forced to undergo an operation necessitated by an infection that developed from broken ribs sustained in the auto accident. But though he still wore the stitches when he appeared at the dinner in his honor, he strode majestically to the platform and stood quietly in a statuesque pose as the gold medal was placed about his neck.

When asked why Top was given his unusual name, his proud owner explained that a friend had given him the choice of an entire litter and that he had selected Top because he was "the top of the whole group." Subsequent events have vindicated his judgment.

TRIXIE

A quick-witted and imaginative mixed breed named Trixie, from Lynn, Massachusetts, was the Dog Hero of the Year for 1971.

The fourth mongrel to win the award but the first whose ancestry was a complete mystery, Trixie used extraordinary intelligence to save her two-year-old master, Ricky Sherry, after the child had tumbled into the icy water of a pond near his home.

Obtained as a puppy from an animal shelter for five dollars three years before, Trixie had led a quiet and placid life as the pet of the Richard Sherry family of Lynn. But on this occasion, when little Ricky managed to squirm through an opening in the fence that enclosed the Sherrys' backyard, Trixie hastened to follow the tyke. It was a cold spring day and the water of Buchanan Bridge Pond stood at thirty-five degrees when the youngster somehow lost his footing on the bank and tumbled into the frigid depths.

Meanwhile, the child's absence had been quickly discovered, and Mrs. Felix Manna, a next-door neighbor, was among those searching for him when she suddenly encountered Trixie, sopping wet and barking loudly and continually. She followed the dog at a run across backyards and weed-covered areas to the water's edge, where Trixie halted, looked up at her, and barked ceaselessly. The woman peered out through the mists but could see nothing.

At this point, Trixie, seeing that her "message" was not being understood, leaped into the icy water, paddled out a short distance, and began swimming in a small circle, barking all the while. Looking closely at the center of the circle, Mrs. Manna finally perceived what turned out to be the tip of the child's aqua-colored jacket, which had blended perfectly with the water. She plunged into the five-foot-deep water and brought the child out.

Firemen responding quickly to the distress call could find no sign of life in the child, although "unbelievable amounts of water" were forced out of his lungs. He was rushed to Lynn Hospital, where a skilled team of physicians waited. With his body temperature standing at only sixty degrees, they were virtually certain that the tot was beyond hope, but nevertheless they utilized every known method of medical science to try to save him.

His body temperature was gradually raised to eighty-three degrees, and suddenly they detected a faint heartbeat, the first in twenty minutes. They kept at their work doggedly, and by noon of the next day, his temperature had returned to normal.

Such an interval between heartbeats had invariably resulted in brain damage in the past, and for an entire week the child was tested and placed under constant observation. Medical history was made when it was discovered that not the slightest mental or physical damage had occurred, and little Ricky was allowed to return home to a wildly enthusiastic Trixie.

MIMI

A miniature Poodle who sounded the alarm when fire broke out and helped to save eight members of a Danbury, Connecticut family was named America's Dog Hero of the Year for 1972.

The dog, Mimi, aroused Mr. Nicholas Emerito at 5:30

A.M. last January after he had dozed off on a sofa after watching the late, late show on television. Awakened by the dog's barking and scratching at his chest, the man found the living room in flames, and smoke throughout the house.

While he ran to waken his wife and small son in a first-floor bedroom, Mimi raced up the stairs and aroused five other children. Although two of the teen-aged boys were trapped by reaching the flaming stairway too late, they leaped to safety from the roof as their father broke their falls. The house was completely destroyed.

BUDWEISER

A Johns Island, South Carolina, St. Bernard named Budweiser, who pulled a four-year-old girl from a blazing house and then returned to rescue a second child, was named America's Dog Hero of 1972.

Budweiser gained hero status when an explosion sent flames shooting through the home of Mr. and Mrs. B. M. Carter, owners of the fourteen-month-old dog. At the time, six of the Carters' grandchildren were in the house with Mrs. Carter. Budweiser charged into the house, grabbed the youngest child, Linda Lawson, by her shirt and pulled her out of the burning home to the safety of a neighbor's yard. He then raced back into the blazing house and pulled five-year-old Joyce Hinson by the arm out of the house and across the yard. In the meantime, Mrs. Carter rounded up the other four children and herded them to safety.

When Budweiser tried to enter the house a third time to rescue the family's Chihuahua, he was driven back by intense flames. Within thirty minutes the roof collapsed and the house was a total loss.

The youngsters who escaped with Mrs. Carter were David, seven; Debby, six; and Billy, five—children of Mr. and Mrs. Lloyd Lawson of Stafford Heights—and Joann, six, daughter of Mr. and Mrs. Frank Hinson of Johns Island.

SKIPPY

A mixed-breed dog who jeopardized his own life to save a six-year-old youngster from a rattlesnake was named America's Dog Hero of 1974.

Skippy, owned by the family of Marine M.Sgt. and Mrs. Gary D. Essig, Santa Ana, California, placed himself between an eighteen-inch rattlesnake poised to strike and Donald, one of his young masters. While saving the young boy's life, the dog incurred the snake's bite and was confined for three days in the intensive care unit at the El Toro Animal Hospital.

For his heroism, Skippy and his owners—including Donald; Mary Ruth, nine; Connie, eight; and their parents—were honored at the twenty-first annual Dog Hero of the Year banquet.

The event that led to Skippy's heroic act occurred on St. Patrick's Day, as the Essig family was breaking up camp after a weekend outing in O'Neill Park, near Santa Ana.

Young Donald, playing in nearby high grass, cried out, "A rattlesnake! A rattlesnake!"

We heard the rattling; it was the loudest noise I ever heard," said Mrs. Essig.

The dog bounded to Donald's aid. Positioning himself between the boy and the rattler, he grabbed the snake between his jaws. Unfortunately, he was too far behind the rattlesnake's head and it was able to turn and strike, piercing the dog's face.

A neighboring camper shot the rattler, and it was then noticed that Skippy's face was starting to swell. The Essigs immediately put the dog into their car and headed to the nearest veterinarian; it was a ten-mile drive and when they reached the nearest animal hospital they found it closed because it was Sunday.

"We dashed to a nearby telephone and phoned one of the hospital's veterinarians, who came over immediately," relates Mrs. Essig.

The dog was given a shot of antivenin and placed in intensive care for three days. He recovered fully.

The Essig family acquired their pet about eight months prior to the accident. "We picked him out of the Orange County Animal Shelter because he looked the saddest," explained Mrs. Essig. "He looked like he was crying; he didn't even bark for quite a long time."

FAWN

A German shepherd who risked a rattlesnake bite to save the life of a three-year-old boy was honored as America's Dog Hero of the Year in 1975.

Owned by Mr. and Mrs. William Schlesinger, St. Petersburg, Florida, Fawn is credited with keeping the Schlesingers' grandson, Russ "Tiger" Schoenberger, out of the path of a rattlesnake. The dog pushed the boy to the ground repeatedly before rushing the snake herself. Fawn suffered a snakebite; the effects lasted four weeks.

The winning dog's owners, Mr. and Mrs. Schlesinger, were surpirsed that Fawn performed so heroically. Normally, she is "shy" and "moody," and does not play with children, primarily acting as a watchdog, they said.

Just before the heroic act occurred, three other family dogs were in the Schlesinger backyard and Fawn was in a screened porch with the Schlesingers, far away from where the child was playing. Apparently sensing the danger, Fawn pushed a screen door open and ran to battle with the rattler, pushing the boy to the ground and fighting with the snake. Schlesinger left the porch to search for a pistol. When he reached the dog and boy, Schlesinger was able to strike the snake with four out of five pistol shots, despite cataracts on his eyes.

"The snake was four feet long but looked ten feet," said Schlesinger. "I acted instinctively to protect a loved one. I did not have time to think."

ZORRO

Zorro, a shepherd-wolf who pulled his unconscious master out of a whirlpool, was honored as America's Dog Hero of the Year for 1976.

Owned by Mr. and Mrs. Mark A. Cooper, Orangevale, California, Zorro is credited with pulling his master out of a whirlpool after Cooper had fallen eighty-five feet into a ravine and been knocked unconscious. The dog slept on top of Cooper during the night to keep him warm while a companion left to find rescuers. Cooper was rescued, but the dog was left behind for want of room. Later, two volunteer searchers from the Sierra Club rescued Zorro, who was still guarding the abandoned backpacking equipment of his master.

The dog's owners were delighted with the news of Zorro's award. "He's a good dog," said Cooper. "I wouldn't be alive today if it wasn't for Zorro."

MEATBALL

Meatball, a German shepherd owned by Mr. and Mrs. Robert Keith of Morris, Alabama, was honored as America's Dog Hero of 1977.

Meatball is credited with interrupting a burglary in progress at the family's greenhouse and trying valiantly to apprehend the culprits. Mrs. Keith was home alone talking to her mother on the phone when she heard someone pick up the extension in the supposedly empty greenhouse behind their home, which is located in a semiremote area. Instead of reaching for a gun, she took Meatball with her to check out the intrusion.

The heroic dog surprised the male intruder and chased him to his getaway car, where an accomplice was waiting. As the would-be burglar jumped into the car, Meatball grabbed his leg and held on firmly while the vehicle sped away. The dog was dragged along the road for several yards and suffered cracked toenails, cut pads on his paws, and a bruised side.

Meatball is also very protective of the Keith's five-year-old daughter, Mary Evelyn. He has been known to take her arm in his mouth and gently lead her away from the street.

CHESSIE

Chester (Chessie), a Chesapeake Bay retriever owned by Mr. and Mrs. Gary Homme of Livingston, Montana, was named the Dog Hero of the Year of 1978.

Chester is credited with pulling five-year-old Kenny Homme from a surging creek that spring. Mrs. Homme was washing dishes at the time. She periodically looked out the kitchen window to check on the boy, who was watering flowers outside. Suddenly Mrs. Homme noticed that Kenny was gone. She ran outside and heard him shouting, "Help me! Save me!"

The boy had slid down a steep hill nearby and had fallen into a creek that was swollen and surging with a powerful current. Chester was in the water trying to save the child. As the dog swam toward Kenny, the water pulled the boy into a culvert. Chester battled the raging water for ten minutes. Kenny grabbed onto Chester's hair twice, but lost his grip both times. Kenny then climbed on top of the dog's back and rode him out of the tunnel to safety. "If we didn't have Chester, we wouldn't have a son right now," Mrs. Homme said.

AND THE RUNNERS-UP...

THUMPER, a German shepherd owned by Mr. James Kennihan of Piedmont, South Dakota, was being boarded for a few days at the kennels in Rapid City operated by Mr. and Mrs. Russel Skog. When the flood of June 9, 1972, hit the town, Mrs. Skog was carried away but was lucky enough to seize Thumper's collar, and the dog kept her afloat until rescuers could reach her more than a half mile from her home.

TARA is a Rottweiler owned by Sandra Ann Stranckmeyer of Quincy, Illinois. When her mother, Mrs. Frances Stranckmeyer, fell in the bathroom early one morning and was bleeding profusely, Tara ran to the girl's room. Although obedience-trained, Tara would not quit barking until the girl got up to investigate. Her mother recovered after thirty-two days of hospitalization.

MICHELLE, is a collie owned by Lester Woods of Everton, Missouri. Woods, a farmer, was attacked by a cow. The cow had just dropped its calf, and the calf's head was twisted under its body. As Woods went to aid it, the cow rushed him, knocked him down, and tried to crush him. Michelle ran to the scene and drove off the animal. Woods was hospitalized four days with a broken collarbone and sprained ankle.

DEE-DOG is a collie owned by Don Perkins of Canyon, Texas. Perkins was badly injured in a fall as he was tending to his nine dogs around midnight on a stormy, near-zero January night. Dee-Dog broke out of his pen and kept the groggy man awake by alternately barking at him and warming him as he crawled the four hundred feet from the kennels to his house. Although suffering badly frostbitten feet, he recovered after hospitalization.

REX, owned by Angela Jones, Davenport, Louisiana, is credited with finding a two-year-old boy trapped in a garbage can. Rex attracted attention by his persistent loud scratching against the metal receptacle, thus saving the youngster's life.

JOE, owned by Mr. and Mrs. Duane Sumpter, Saratoga Springs, New York, grabbed the arm of the couple's son and *held him above water* for ten minutes until rescuers were able to reach them.

DUKE, a collie owned by Mr. and Mrs. William Fugate, of Brookfield, Missouri, alerted the couple to a tornado heading directly toward their farm. The couple had no storm cellar and drove out of the path of the twister, which devastated their farm.

GIDGET is a Poodle who violated training rules by climbing stairs to the second floor of the owner's house to alert a young boy to a fire burning below. The boy carried his ninety-one-year-old grandmother to safety. The Poodle is owned by Dr. and Mrs. Howard Krause of Warren, Ohio.

RED, an Irish Setter owned by Mr. and Mrs. Bruce R. Morris, St. Charles, Missouri, adopted only three weeks before, saved the Morrises' two-year-old daughter, Margaret, from a burning automobile moments before it was engulfed by fire and gutted.

DAISY MAE, a two-year-old Leopard Hound owned by Terry Legatti, Belleair, Florida, brought help to neighbor Arthur Aikin who broke his hip in a fifteen-foot fall from a ladder while trimming a tree.

QUEENIE, a Doberman pinscher owned by Mr. and Mrs. William Goerlitz, Jr., of Jacksonville, Florida, protected Mrs. Goerlitz and her two-year-old daughter, Emerald, from a rattlesnake that was lurking in a tool shed.

JEFFERSON, an Irish Setter owned by Mr. and Mrs. James Fitzpatrick and their nine children of Highland, Indiana, saved sixteen-year-old Margaret Fitzpatrick from electrocution near the family's backyard swimming pool.

ROMMEL, A Bouvier des Flandres puppy owned by Mr. and Mrs. Terry Sheeran of Rochester, Michigan, saved two-year-old Kelly McDonough of Royal Oak, Michigan, from drowning in a four-foot-deep well.

DUKE, a German shepherd owned by Mr. and Mrs. Calvin Richardson of Finksburg, Maryland, saved four-year-old Timmy Richardson from being bitten by a deadly copperhead snake.

LADY, a German shepherd from Ormond Beach, Florida, stood guard over five small girls lost in a forest for eighteen hours. KING, a husky from South Boston, Massachusetts, alerted his sleeping master to a fire in his home. CINDY was a German shepherd from Phoenix,

Arizona, whose excited barks brought a mother to the rescue of her twenty-two-month-old son, who had fallen into a neighbor's swimming pool. SMOKEY, a mixed breed from New Britain, Connecticut, helped save the lives of thirteen people by barking an alarm when fire swept their three-flat residence.

CHAPTER FOUR

CIRCUS HEROES

People who operate circuses are often unwilling to relate stories in which animals have come to the rescue of humans, for this implies that things can go wrong at the circus. But whether or not the circus folk will own up to it, things can and do go wrong on occasion. Fortunately, it does not happen often. When it does, the only thing between a human and an animal bent on destruction is another animal.

Tom Cathro is employed by one of this country's major circuses, and while he was willing to have his name mentioned, he asked that the name of the circus with which he is connected be withheld. His wishes have of course been respected. He has provided the very interesting stories in this chapter.

The reader may be assured that while names have been changed, all of these stories are true.

There are two basic kinds of circus acts involving cats. There's the "love act," in which the trainer and the big felines appear to be in love with each other, and the "fighting act," in which the trainer seems to control the big cats with chairs, whips, clubs, and guns. The cats pretend to hate the trainer, they snarl, paw, and growl. It's a frightening thing to watch.

However, in every cat act there's one cat who, whether it's a fighting act or a love act, seems to be in love with the trainer. This one special cat will allow the trainer to punch her, tickle her, fondle her, maul or pet her, and will even suffer herself to be lifted and draped over the trainer's shoulders.

One of the worst things that can happen in the cage is to have a female cat in heat. When a male becomes aware of this, his own instincts will throw all discipline and training to the winds. If the trainer dares to get between him and the female, he will only compound the problems.

This is exactly what happened during an afternoon performance at a major circus. One of the female cats was in heat, and a big male decided to investigate the matter. He left his pedestal and headed for the female. The handler stepped between him and the female and tried to herd him back to his place. The big cat was having none of this. He advanced toward the female, bypassing the handler. The handler again stepped between them, and the big male cat turned full toward the trainer, snarled, curled his lip, and growled a growl that came from the depths of his deep, barrel-like chest.

The trainer did all that he could. He cracked his whip, attempted to face the lion down, fired the blank cartridge pistol, all to no avail. That male lion had a one-track mind and would not be dissuaded. The trainer stood his ground. The lion, realizing that first things had to come first, turned his full attention to the trainer. He tilted his head to one side, opened his huge maw, and, screaming a challenge, raised one paw. The stroke felled the trainer, who dropped to the sawdust of the cage, blood spurting from his chest. Seeing the trouble in the cage, the bandleader struck up a military march. The audience sat silently, watching the drama playing out before their eyes. Outside the cage, one of the assistants threw a shell into the big-bore Winchester and prepared to fire a round at the cat. The big lion, having tasted blood, forgot about the female and concentrated only on completing his kill.

Slowly, the big cat circled the supine man, working himself into sufficient frenzy to leap in and complete the destruction of the handler. But suddenly, something changed in the cage. For standing between the fallen man and his four-legged adversary was the "love cat." She faced the male down, standing steadfastly and giving no ground. She raised a paw menacingly, claws fully extended. The male saw that she meant business and hesitated in his advance. Slowly, the assistant handler lowered his rifle, waiting to see what would happen. He knew that the big cats were expensive and that to destroy one when there was any other alternative would be horribly wasteful.

The big lion continued a slow retreat, as though he had simply changed his mind—almost a sort of face-saving gesture. The lioness still did not move.

Suddenly, the big male turned, wheeling on his two hind legs, and rushed almost the full length of the cage directly at the lioness, trying to frighten her away under the force of his attack. She snarled, raised her paw again, and laid her ears back against her head. The lion pulled up short, stopping his attack in front of the lioness.

Now she glared at the other cats in the cage, daring them to make a move. As she met the eyes of each, each turned his head away.

She licked the handler's face and then turned toward the door of the cage, stepping aside and placing herself between the man and the other cats, as though to tell the assistants outside the cage that it was all right to come in now. They did—and removed the wounded man. Now the door to the escape tunnel was open, and the lioness helped the assistant handler herd the cats through the tunnel. Then with a last over-the-shoulder look, she turned and bounded up the ramp herself.

The trainer recovered and was soon back at work in the ring. However, there's a slight change now in the activities inside the cage. He carries a bit of liver with him and at the end of every show, the "love cat" gets that small treat. She always thanks him with a big, wet lick along the side of his face!

Where animals are concerned, another type of problem occasionally arises. Animals can—for no apparent reason—go berserk. Elephants, especially, can become "rogue" and will from then on be totally unmanageable. They destroy anything that gets in their way, rampaging and trumpeting. It's like a human being having a total nervous breakdown.

When an elephant runs amok like this, the usual procedure is to lash him to a large, calm elephant and then try to lead both to a sturdy tree. The wild one is then lashed to the tree, and the calm elephant is released. At this point, the rogue elephant can be destroyed.

However, elephants are not cheap, and when one does go sour, the circus tries everything else before destroying such a valuable property. The vet will inject tranquilizers in the hope that the big beast will calm down. When all else fails, there's one last ploy—to donate it to a local zoo that may be happy to have a live elephant. In fact, the circus can even make a deal with the zoo to provide a letter of thanks; that letter becomes a nice tax deduction the following year!

You may have heard the old saying, "Elephants never forget." That just happens to be true, and while an elephant never forgets a wrong, it will also remember a kindness.

Elephants, whether male or female, are called "bulls" in circus parlance, and Bingo was a big African cow who came to the timely rescue of her handler. In case you're not familiar with circus lore, elephant handlers are called "mahout," which is pronounced "may-out." Bill, the handler at this circus, loved the big beasts and was always with them on the back lot, either scrubbing them down or giving them haircuts. Oh, yes! Elephants do indeed grow hair, which feels like the bristles on a brush. Bill trimmed the elephants' hair with a fast-moving blowtorch. This is standard practice and doesn't hurt the beasts at all.

The problem came when Bill was scrubbing down an old bull who suddenly, for no apparent reason, went mad. He spread his huge, fanlike ears, raised his trunk, became wild-eyed, and after trumpeting a warning, turned on Bill. Bill wasn't so much angry as scared. The other elephants, realizing what was happening, tried to get away. So did Bill, and before long, the place was a melee of frightened, stampeding elephants, with Bill right in the middle of the mess. Trying to avoid the thundering and ponderous beasts, Bill headed toward the bars of the cage, hoping he could work his way around to the door. Ordinarily, there's more than ample room for a man to get out between the bars of an elephant cage, but this was not the case today. Bill was inside the cage with the elephants, and there was no place to go as one of the big beasts leaned against him, pressing him against the bars. Bill feared that the next step would be a horrible, crushing death.

But such was not the case. The elephant holding him to the bars was Bingo, one of Bill's good friends. She saw the situation and realized that Bill was in jeopardy. She stood between him and the attacking bull, so that Bill was protected by her body.

Bill talked to Bingo, calming her, trying to mask the fear in his own voice. Under his direction, she slowly edged around the periphery of the cage, closer and closer to the door. The maddened bull screamed his frustration, pawing at the ground, but totally unable to get at the man.

Finally, they reached the door and Bill got out of the cage. Along with his helpers, he calmed the bull, administered a tranquilizer, and things again settled down.

Bingo was rewarded for her act of heroism in ways that elephants understand. She was thanked by Bill personally and rewarded with an extra tidbit at mealtimes. There's a new bond between Bill and Bingo, and in addition to a treat whenever Bill thinks of it, there's always a friendly pat for the big beast from the man whose life she helped save.

Did you know that all of the members of the ape family are afraid of clowns? It's quite true. It doesn't matter whether it's a small rhesus monkey or a full-grown gorilla. You'll rarely see monkeys working around the clowns or vice-versa.

Sol is a clown who is getting along in years. On one

particular summer day, Sol had finished his stint under the big top and was heading back to clown alley to remove his makeup and costume. It was a hot, exhausting day, and as Sol walked back, he had a heart attack. He clutched his chest as the pain ripped through him, racing up his left arm. He was unable to breathe. He sank slowly to his knees, and, as he fell face down on the ground, he blacked out.

During this time, Charley, the ape handler, was collecting his charges and getting them ready for the next show. Jeff, a small chimpanzee, took advantage of the situation and got away from Charley and headed around the back of the big tent. Charley wasn't very worried about it, for Jeff was well trained, and when his name was called, he'd surely show up. Besides, Jeff knew his way around the lot. He was a friendly ape and everybody liked him. Charley shook his head and continued on his way. He simply figured he'd go after Jeff later on.

In the course of Jeff's escape, his travels took him around the back of the tent where Sol lay. Jeff stopped in his tracks and stared at the unconscious man's form, crooning lowly to himself, almost as if debating what to do. He approached carefully, perhaps wondering if this was not some kind of trick that Charley was playing on him. Then he saw Sol's face, covered with the white makeup and bulbous red plastic nose. Jeff jumped back in horror. He began chattering wildly, bounding about, now retreating, now advancing with one paw raised menacingly.

Charley began looking for Jeff, angry to have to take the time to seek the monkey out. He called again and again, but Jeff did not respond.

Suddenly, Jeff appeared from behind the tent. "There you are!" Charley said. He held his arms forward, beckoning Jeff to come to him. Instead, Jeff jabbered excitedly and disappeared behind the tent, appearing a moment later to see if Charley was following. Naturally, Charley was angry now. As Charley rounded the corner of the tent, he saw Jeff squatting about six feet away from Sol. Charley quickly summoned help, and scant moments later, an ambulance arrived with a medical team that rushed Sol to the hospital.

Sol recovered. He is now semiretired, living near the circus' winter quarters, where he can keep a fist in and help the younger clowns with their routines. He's also made a personal pet of Jeff. They're together all of the time, for Sol is convinced that the ape saved his life. And Jeff? He's earned that place in Sol's affections, for he overcame his inborn fear and knew that there was a man under that ridiculous suit and that dead-white makeup. He stayed, called, and waited until a human came to render the assistance that saved Sol's life.

Incidentally, Sol tried putting on the clown makeup while Jeff sat on a nearby table and watched. Sol hoped that by seeing the white go on, he'd know that his friend Sol was under it. But it didn't help a bit. Jeff still hates the whiteface!

Bears may look nice and cuddly, but if you ever watch a bear act, you'll notice that the bears are all muzzled. Bears' looks are deceiving, and those muzzles should show you how professional bear handlers feel about their charges. Visitors to Yellowstone National Park are always cautioned against feeding bears, for in spite of the cute and colorful cartoon characters seen on television, bears are not terribly selective. While they'll willingly eat out of your hand, they'll keep right on eating, even after the food is gone!

The natural position for bears is on all fours. The only time they stand erect is when ready for a fight. The fact that dancing bear acts require the bear to be standing erect is an invitation for trouble.

At one show, the bear handler's wife was supposed to dance with a big brown bear. She had done this often before and did not anticipate any fateful consequences on this particular afternoon. The band was playing a slow waltz, and the handler's wife was dancing with the bear, his big paws draped over her shoulders. Finally, he decided that he had had enough. He let her know that he was tired of dancing by raking at her with a big paw, claws fully extended. She toppled to the floor of the cage, bleeding profusely from the gashes. Then she fainted. Before anybody could do anything, the big bear turned to the attack again.

Another bear in the troupe dropped from its pedestal. The handlers feared a panic in the ring, with all the animals getting out of hand. But this second bear dashed across the ring to the limp woman's body and took a position straddling her.

The first bear seemed to think that the second bear was challenging it for its kill. It slowly circled, growling menacingly, looking for a way to retrieve the woman. The second bear, Igor, kept turning to face the attacker and returned growl for growl.

Fear gripped the others in the troupe. It looked as if two bears were going to fight for the woman. Igor rose to his hind legs, paws up, challenging the first bear. The first bear got the message and turned away as though no longer interested.

The handlers fully expected the big Igor to administer a crushing blow and devour the woman. Instead, Igor looked around at them and began yelping like a puppy. He stepped aside to allow the handlers to come forward to rescue the woman.

It took a bit of hurry-up medical attention and a little plastic surgery, but the woman is back with the troupe now, and while she still doesn't fully trust the big beasts, she is nonetheless able to work with them. "I don't know for sure if Igor was just trying to steal the attacking bear's kill and thought better of it or if he was really trying to save my life," she says. But at feeding time, she always has an extra little treat for Igor and a carefully administered pat on the head!

You've probably seen elephants moving in what is called a "chain line." The second elephant holds the tail of the first elephant in his trunk and so on down the chain. Why are elephants moved about in a chain line? Because it's the easiest way to handle them in an orderly fashion. And why do the elephants do it? Because they've been trained to. They know that if they break the chain or get out of the line, they'll feel the bull hook in a most sensitive portion of their anatomy.

The mahout was taking the elephants from the barn to the show ring, leading the chain. Everything was quite normal, and the elephants were behaving in their usual docile fashion. But then an unusual thing happened. Gertie, a big African elephant, dropped the tail of her leader and headed toward an area behind the midway. The other elephants in the string stopped, wondering what to do. The mahout stopped, too. He didn't know whether to chase Gertie, which would mean leaving his other charges, or stay with the herd. He followed Gertie with his eyes and began to holler for help.

Gertie had obviously seen something. She headed right for it, too. What she saw was a knock-down, drag-out fist fight between one of the circus roughnecks and a local. There had been a discussion of whether or not a ticket had been bought for one of the midway attractions, and the discussion got hotter and hotter until the two went out back. The two were really going at it, and that's when Gertie spotted the imbroglio and plunged toward the two men. When she got there, she pushed them apart with her trunk and stood between them, trumpeting wildly, in the full knowledge that this would attract assistance.

It did. Help arrived, the men were separated, and the local police department came and collected both of them. They were sent in to cool off for a while. And Gertie? She allowed herself to be led back to the chain line, where she took her place again and continued the march into the ring.

One of the attractions at a small circus was a huge tank that housed acrobatic underwater animals.

A very young child was peering over the edge of the tank during the between–show period when he toppled into the water. The tot couldn't swim, and the child's mother screamed frantically for help. Help was on the way, and one of the keepers had already removed his sneakers in preparation to dive into the tank. On the walkway around the tank, the child's mother was nearly fainting.

Suddenly, two black shapes appeared just below the surface of the water. They sped toward the baby, and then, one at a time, swam under the child's limp form and raised it to the surface. By continuing the process, they were able to keep the child afloat and breathing until the other keeper arrived with a large hook that was caught under the boy's clothing. The child was pulled to safety.

This was an overt act of heroism, for the porpoises—the black shapes in the tank—realized that without their direct help the child would drown.

You've probably seen the hard and heavy work that the roughnecks and roustabouts do when a tent show pulls into a new town. There's a lot of strong-arm work required, and time is always limited. The object is to get things ready overnight so the show can go on the next day. Because most of the acts want to make sure that their equipment is properly installed, they usually do the installation work themselves. Tightwire acts will erect their own wires and towers. The aerialists—at the very least—supervise the erection of their own equipment. At the end of the day, what you have is sore and aching muscles, blistered and tired hands, and a thoroughly worn-out work gang.

One night, a fire broke out. To a tent show, fire is anathema, for it can wipe out a circus completely. It was the first night in a new town for the show. The circus people were dog tired, and everybody was fast asleep. Suddenly, the seals started barking, just like dogs, carrying on a raucous chatter. Seals are usually very quiet, and the seal trainer got out of bed to see what the trouble was.

He saw the flames and gave the alarm. Fortunately, only one small sideshow tent had been affected, and the fire was extinguished in sufficient time to prevent its spread. After the fire was out, everybody went back to bed once again, slept late the next morning—and then got up in time to clean up the mess, put up a new tent, and open the show on schedule.

The seals that gave the original alarm were never in danger, for their tank was sufficiently far from the fire to be quite safe. By barking and waking the trainer, their only motive could have been concern for the well-being of man. Their own lives were never in jeopardy, and their in-time warning saved the show a great loss, for had the fire spread, as it must have done had it not been confined in time, all would have been lost.

When a circus travels between towns, the traveling is done by rail if it's a really big show. Most of the smaller circuses travel by road in an assortment of trucks, vans, cars, and wheeled cages. With the enormous mileage covered by these shows, it isn't unusual for accidents to take place.

A typical small circus was on the road between towns when one of the drivers pulled up for a rest stop. By the time he got back on the road, the rest of the column had gone on ahead of him. In his truck were a group of elephants, and the elephant handler was sleeping on a shelf bed behind the cab of the van.

The driver expected to catch up with the column farther down the road. Other drivers waved as they went by. He shifted his weight in the seat to make himself more comfortable and kept his eyes on the road ahead, just in front of the splash of light from his headlights. Occasionally, he'd glance ahead, trying to locate the column. He watched as his speedometer climbed to slightly above the normal cruising speed of the big truck. He felt that by holding at an accelerated speed, he'd overtake the column before they reached the next town.

Then it happened. The road turned, and the truck didn't. It plunged over the side of the road and down an embankment. The cab plowed into a huge tree, instantly killing the driver. The truck tumbled and overturned. The back of the big rig broke open, and the elephants clambered out. With no place to go, they stood around and waited.

The elephant handler was trapped on the bed behind the cab. He was pinned down by one of the truck's structural members and could not free himself. Both his legs were fractured and he was unable to move. He was fully conscious and in great pain. He feared that fire would break out while

103

he was trapped. He could smell the stench of raw gasoline as it flowed from the ruptured fuel lines.

Turning his head, he saw the elephants standing there. He called to them. They turned their heads and looked. That was the last thing he remembered before he blacked out.

At the next town, the circus had arrived and was setting up. Somebody remembered that the elephant truck had never caught up with them. A pickup truck was dispatched to see what the problem was. It backtracked along the same road, going slowly, keeping an eye out for the missing truck. The roustabout who was driving the truck and his two companions couldn't believe the sight that greeted them as they rounded a turn. Off the road was the wrecked truck, the dead driver, and all the elephants, standing patiently, awaiting further orders.

All the elephants except for one. One big female was poised over the cab of the truck holding a large metal beam in her trunk. The body of the handler lay below. Nobody could tell how long she had stayed in that position, holding the heavy beam away from the handler's body. The men quickly pulled him free, carrying him to the bed of the pickup truck. They then instructed the elephant to drop the beam. She did so, turned, and walked to join the other elephants. One man stayed at the scene while the others rushed back to town to get the handler to the hospital. They came back the next day with another truck to get the elephants.

Naturally, in any circus, you're going to have a lot of elephant stories. Elephants have an excellent sense of humor, and their thinking is often similar to that of man. As a result, amusing situations often arise.

Circuses are often prey to less-than-ethical townspeople, for circus folk are all out-of-towners and may be considered fair pickings for local crooks. The modern-day crooks usually realize that the "office truck" is where all the circus receipts are collected. One enterprising local, a young man, decided to rob the truck. He entered the office truck armed with a pistol, a bandanna over his face, looking like a modern Jesse James.

Inside the truck was a silent alarm that had been tripped when he entered. But that wasn't all. As the youth backed out the door, pistol in one hand, money in the other, he was met by a huge African elephant that quickly snaked her trunk around his upper torso, pinning his arms to his sides. He hadn't seen the elephant waiting for him and was taken totally by surprise. To say he was frightened would be the understatement of the year. After all, how would you feel if you backed into the trunk of a huge pachyderm and were lifted twelve feet into the air?

The man screamed, but to no avail. He dropped the pistol and was then gently relieved of the money by the man who had been summoned by the alarm. The money was returned to the office truck and counted. The local sheriff was sent for. When he arrived, he looked at the situation, took off his hat and scratched his head. He took the culprit into custody, for the big elephant released the man when ordered to do so.

A local newspaper reporter, summoned by the show's publicity man, arrived on the scene with his camera and set up a series of posed photographs. The one that made the newspapers showed the sheriff pinning his own badge on the elephant's halter and naming her a special deputy!

If you've ever seen a full three-ring circus, you know that there's a lot of activity going on all the time. At one show, there was an equestrian act in the center ring, and high above, the trapeze artists were working. In this particular show, no nets were used. The flyers were the main focus of attention, and the spotlights were on them.

In the sawdust, the horses were being put through their paces by their trainer. He competed with the other acts by cracking the whip noisily to call attention to his own act. As it happened on this fateful day, attention was called to his act from an unexpected quarter and in an unexpected way.

One of the most spectacular numbers in the aerial act was a one-and-one-half somersault with a twist performed by a young female artiste. She stood poised on the high perch, timing the back-and-forth swings of her catcher. Now he turned, dropped to hang from his knees, and extended his arms. She threw her own trapeze one time, caught it on its return, and then, holding on with both hands, swung from the perch.

She and the catcher sailed toward each other. They swung outward once more, and this time, as they approached, she released the bar of her trapeze, did her twist and somersault in midair, and reached for his wrists. Their hands touched. Suddenly, to the horror of all who saw, she slipped and plummeted to the floor of the tent.

What happened next, happened very quickly. While almost everybody was horror-struck, one mind thought quickly and acted on that thought. The mind that saved her life was not the mind of a human, but that of a brave horse.

The horse, a part of the equestrian team, saw the girl lose her grip and fall. Quickly, he broke out of his easy-loping circular pattern around the ring and darted to where he thought the girl would hit ground. He braced his legs, head turned upward. The girl's body hit the horse, knocking him to the ground. He rolled under the force of the impact, and the girl, after hitting the horse, dropped to the ground. When help finally arrived, she was unconscious but only had the wind knocked out of her. Thanks to the quick-witted selfless action of the horse, her life was spared. The horse quickly snorted and regained his feet, none the worse for the experience.

One of the things that attracts people to a circus is the element of danger. Only a small wire grille protects you from a wild beast; only his skill and daring protects the trainer from the same beast. And one of the things that is most dreaded in a circus is the escape of a wild animal. In instances where this has occurred, the danger is usually not the result of contact with the animal but the ensuing panic that can cause trampling and other injuries.

At a small midwestern circus, such an incident took place. The cat show had finished, and all of the big cats were supposed to have exited through the escape tunnel and up the ramp. After the tunnel had been closed, the gaffers pulled the ropes, raising the cage to the top of the tent where it would be out of the way. The next act was an equestrian team. It took but a moment for the roustabouts to clear away the cat pedestals, and the horses and handlers were already waiting at the entrance. It was a fast change and all was in readiness.

Nobody seemed to notice the tiger that crouched behind one of the pedestals. The cat handler had taken his last bow, and at that point, one of the roustabouts discovered the cat and shouted an alarm. Then he got out of there fast. The others followed suit.

The horse troupe was ready to enter, and was therefore blocking the only viable exit for the big cat.

People in the audience do what people in audiences usually do at times like this. They screamed. The big cat, frightened by its sudden freedom and the rush of activity, ran toward the entrance to the tent, where the equestrians were waiting.

The female handler, seeing what was happening, wanted to make her own escape but was torn by a need to protect her charges. She knew that tigers have no compunctions about destroying horses. The tiger stealthily moved about, waiting for his chance. The girl suddenly screamed, and that triggered all the action that took place in the next moments. It happened so quickly that varying versions of what actually transpired have appeared. As nearly as I can piece together, here's what actually happened.

Hearing the girl's scream, the frightened tiger lunged toward her. Two of the horses turned and escaped back out the tent's entrance. The girl fell fainting to the sawdust. One of the horses, seeing the girl lying there, the tiger rapidly approaching, turned back again and positioned himself between the girl's body and the tiger, now in full attack.

At the crucial moment, and with timing that was worthy of a championship boxer, the horse reared, his forelegs flailing at the air, and he caught the tiger under the chin with one of his hooves. Contact was perfect. The tiger went limp and crumpled to a heap in the sawdust, scant inches from the girl's body. The horse, now thoroughly frightened, reared again. He was stopped and calmed by one of the equestrian handlers, then led wild-eyed away from the scene. The unconscious tiger was carried from the ring after having been bound and muzzled. His broken jaw had to be set by the circus veterinarian.

The tiger recovered and continues to perform with the circus, but his activities have changed. He's undergone another step in his training. When the escape tunnel door opens, he's the first cat out of the performance cage. There's no way that he will, after his last experience, remain behind again! He's also developed a healthy respect for, and a deadly fear of, horses!

Elephants are draft animals, and while they certainly are circus curiosities, they serve as beasts of burden when they are not being shown or put through their paces.

When a circus enters a small town, it often performs what is called the "circus parade." This did not start out as a planned organized parade as such, but rather the simplest means of moving the circus and its equipment through the town to the lot where the show will take place. The curious scene of wild beasts moving through town always attracted a crowd of onlookers, and it wasn't long before the "parade" evolved into an excellent publicity stunt. Clowns were in full makeup, the calliope played, the band performed, and all the other circus performers were in costume.

In one such parade, elephants were used as draft animals to pull the animal cages, the bandwagon, and the calliope wagon. The parade moved through the town at a slow pace, giving the locals an excellent chance to see what they could expect if they bought a ticket.

Suddenly, the steam calliope came to a halt. The elephant refused to take another step. The mahout prodded, coaxed, cajoled, all to no avail. That elephant wasn't about to budge. Other handlers started calling and then came forward to assist in getting the big beast moving. People on the sidelines began wise-cracking, saying things like "That elephant must have some mule in her!" It almost seemed true, for the elephant wouldn't budge, standing steadfastly and resolutely in place.

This was strange behavior indeed for this particular beast, who was ordinarily docile and tractable. How could she know that there was danger ahead? Danger in the form of a fallen electric line that had landed in the water of the streets, recently wet from a severe rainfall. To move forward would mean stepping into the water on the street, water alive with sufficient current to kill her and all those who were in contact with any of the metal parts of the wagon.

Then one of the men saw sparks as the wind swept the end of the wire into and out of the water. Help was summoned and the wire was repaired. The elephant then proceeded as though nothing at all had happened. Surely, whatever instincts came into play had saved the elephant's life—and the lives of several men as well.

One of the things that all animals fear is fire. You may have simply shrugged off seeing an animal leap through a burning hoop, but when you stop to consider that the animal has overcome a basic, deathly fear to learn this trick, it takes on monumental importance.

Horses seem to have a special fear when it comes to flame, for while they are as frightened of it as other animals are, they react even more wildly. Theirs is not so much fear as abject terror.

At the particular circus in question, there was another unusual thing about the horses. They had a pet! This is not at all unusual. Most racehorses have a small dog, a "familiar," if you will, who shares the stable space and is always around the horse. The small dog is a friend, a companion, in other words—a pet.

The horse areas around a circus are fire hazards. Straw and hay are tinder-dry.

One night at this small circus, the barn tent went up in flames. The blaze spread so rapidly that it could almost be called an explosion. The horses, heard whinnying in panic inside, were doomed, for their handlers could not get into the flaming area to save them. Several tried, soaking their coats and holding the wet coats over their heads. But to no avail. They emerged, one after the other, empty-handed, choking on the fumes.

Maybe it's because heat and gases rise, and dogs are built lower to the ground. Maybe. But as the equestrian team stood in horror, waiting helplessly while their horses burned, the horses' pet dog ran into the flaming structure. His barks were easily audible. Before long, he emerged, coming out backward, dragging a horse through the smoke and flame, his teeth clenched on the horse's halter and lead. His coat was smoldering. Men rushed up to relieve him of the halter, leading the horse to safety.

Before he could be stopped, the dog lurched back into the flames. Again he appeared, leading a second horse. This act of total bravery was repeated again and again until all the horses were saved. The dog was more dead than alive, burned by falling coals and choking on the noxious vapors.

Finally, when the last horse had been led to safety, the dog was taken by firemen to a nearby truck where an impromptu oxygen tent was rigged. Soon after, he had fully recovered.

There are two types of wire walkers in the circus—the tightrope walker and the slack-wire artiste. The slack wire is permitted to swing and sway as the performer does his work. The tightrope is just that—tight.

The usual rigging for a tightrope act consists of towers between which the wire is suspended, plus a series of anchors which hold the ends of the wire. Turnbuckles are used to tighten the wire by pulling against the anchors.

At one circus, the rigging was erected and the turnbuckles tightened. What was not seen until too late was that one of the anchors had pulled out, loosened sufficiently so that the high-wire walker who had been planning a tightrope act was now inadvertently doing a slack wire act. As he performed, the anchor pulled out more and more, and he shouted to the ground for help.

One of the roustabouts heard him and saw what was happening. He grabbed a tent stake and tried to tighten the turnbuckle. All he succeeded in doing, however, was to pull the anchor out faster.

At about the same time, the elephants had completed their act and were exiting the tent. One of them, Big Sue, saw and heard. She was almost out of the tent when suddenly she wheeled about and headed for the anchor rope. She twisted her trunk around the wire and pulled. The wire was suddenly taut once again. The wire walker, seeing what had happened, and feeling the rope grow taut under his feet, headed back to the opposite platform to make his escape. Then he realized that Big Sue was not going to let go. Daringly, he ventured slowly back toward the center of the wire. He tested the tightness with his legs. Satisfied that Big Sue was the best anchor he had ever had, he proceeded to complete his act.

When the act was over, the band struck up a rousing tune. The spotlights played on the wire walker, and he took his bow at the center of the rope. Then he gestured to the ground at his side, and one of the spotlights picked up Big Sue. The audience cheered, and Big Sue, in spite of being a ham, refrained from taking a bow herself.

Spectators insist on doing stupid things at circuses. At one circus, a sideshow was set up with the animal cages in long rows so that the people could walk by and look at the various wild animals. A fence was set up to separate the people from the cages by a good four feet. A group of people stopped in front of the lion cage. One of the men, apparently unhappy about the fact that the lion was simply lying on the floor of the cage, decided to prod him into some activity by poking at the helpless beast with his walking stick. The lion, not very happy about this, got up and moved farther back in the cage.

The foolhardy man, not willing to be outfoxed by a lion, climbed over the barrier so he could get closer to the lion with his stick. His friends egged him on, and he assumed the role of a "lion tamer," shouting words that he thought a lion tamer should shout. He attacked the lion with the stick, jabbing at him and striking him. The lion, very annoyed at this point, seized the stick in his jaws and yanked it from the man's hands, dropping it to the floor of the cage. Having disarmed his adversary, he again retreated to an out-of-reach point in the cage.

The lion wasn't looking for trouble, and if the man had simply walked away at this point, nothing more would have happened. But he couldn't leave matters alone. He attempted to retrieve his cane. He reached inside the cage. The lion, thinking that he was being subjected to further attack, reached out with a massive paw and raked the man's arm, ripping his jacket, his shirt, and his arm. Blood gushed from the arm, and he howled in pain. His screams and the screams of his friends soon brought the handlers to the scene. One of them had a small chimpanzee on his shoulder, and the chimp quickly squeezed between the bars of the cage, screaming and moving very quickly. The lion, following the chimp, then released the man and moved after the chimp to the back of the cage. The chimp quickly jumped to the bars at the top of the cage and again drew the lion's attention from the man. Before leaving the lion cage, the chimp recovered the walking stick, and tossed that out of the cage, too.

This story did not end here. The irate man, having suffered pain and bloodshed at the paws of the wild beast, was sent to a hospital, where he was treated and then released. However, he brought suit against the circus for damages. The trial was most interesting. His friends appeared on his behalf and explained that the lion, unprovoked, had attacked him mercilessly. The story, as they told it to his attorney—and as the attorney related to the court—was one of total carelessness on the part of the circus.

But the attorney for the circus brought out a few salient facts, such as the damage to the walking stick, the length of the man's arms and the length of the stick, and the width of the lion cage. It became patently obvious that the man had gone behind the guardrail to taunt the beast and that he had provoked the attack.

The circus filed a countersuit against the man to recover the damages for the bad publicity, for medical costs that they had assumed on his behalf, and for the risk to the chimpanzee's life. What happened in the courtroom was almost a comedy, for under cross-examination, the man owned up, piece by piece, to everything he had done. The judge decided that the circus had taken ample precautions. He threw the man's case out of court and awarded damages to the circus to defray the costs it had incurred.

CHAPTER FIVE

HEROIC PETS

Not all heroic pets receive the accolades they deserve. Sometimes the rewards fall far short of what might be expected.

Dogs are often characterized by the so-called characteristics of their breed. Many dogs get a "bad press" and a reputation that they do not deserve, simply because they belong to a particular breed. For example, Doberman pinschers are supposed to be vicious, and while some of them—those that have been trained for attack—may well be, others are as sweet and friendly as you could want a dog to be.

Doris is a young lady who asked if she could come with me to a training session at the Manhattan Obedience Training School for Dogs. Before she started up the stairs, she asked if there would be any Doberman pinschers there, as she was deathly afraid of that breed. She was told that there might be but was assured that the dogs were well behaved.

There were just two empty seats, both up front and, as luck would have it, a Dobie named Crystal was sitting with her mistress in one of the adjacent seats. Naturally, I took the chair next to the dog, who promptly looked at me and began to sniff. I extended one hand, palm down, and allowed her to get acquainted with me. Then when she raised her nose to my mouth, I exhaled a bit so she could smell my breath. Dogs seem to feel more comfortable after such ceremonies.

Doris watched all this with great fear. She sat as far from Crystal as she could. The dog's mistress kept Crystal on a short lead. When Doris realized that she wouldn't be eaten alive by this vicious animal, she extended a hand, and she and Crystal got better acquainted. It wasn't long before Crystal was standing in front of Doris, her paws on Doris's lap, licking Doris's face! Doris quickly revised her opinion of "all" Dobies.

Dogs are extremely sensitive to emotional reaction in humans. If you show fear, the dog will sense this and react by simply assuming that you've done something to be afraid of. He'll be—at the very least—suspicious of you.

German shepherds are lovely, intelligent dogs, but they are referred to as "police dogs" or "guard dogs" and are often condemned unfairly.

By the same token, not all Old English sheepdogs are clowns, not all Bearded Collies are just "made of love," and not all terriers are "impossible to train."

What *does* make up a dog's personality is the attitude he sees in the people around him. If his family offers lots of love and affection to each other and to him, he will respond in kind, whatever his breed.

Unfortunately, all sorts of unfair stories crop up. One case, for instance, involved a large St. Bernard who attacked, bit, and killed the young son of its master. This story got a wide press, and was fodder for the tabloids for weeks. The dog was put to death, and in an effort to investigate the cause of the dog's "turning" on the child, X rays were taken of the dog's head. Perhaps the veterinarian expected to find a blood clot that might have affected the dog's brain. What he found was a ball-point pen inserted deeply into the dog's ear—cause enough to bite anybody. I know I'd bite, and probably a lot more, if you tried to stick a pen into my ear!

When a dog does do something that is heroic, when he actually can be credited with saving human lives, the chances are that he will have secured a place for himself in the affections of his family forever. Right? Not always. This was not the case with Rocky, a German shepherd in Jersey City, New Jersey.

Fire broke out in Rocky's home, and it was his barking that led to the rescue of the five members of his family, people who otherwise would have perished in the flames.

Then the family moved to California. And Rocky? Oh, the dog? The hero who had saved their lives? Well, they weren't certain that they'd be able to get a place to live out there if Rocky were along, so they deserted him. He finally found himself at the Humane Society, up for adoption.

This is a horrible thing to do to any animal and is especially horrible to a German shepherd, who has great difficulty in transferring his affections. Shepherds are usually "one-man" dogs and will even go so far as to attach themselves to a single family member. And bear in mind that the shepherd is just that—a shepherd. His breeding and background require that he have his entire flock together— his family—before he can so much as sleep easily at night.

The story ends happily, though, for Janet Becker of the Humane Society put out a call, and the Mazzaro family responded. They adopted Rocky and were adopted by him. As of the last reports, Rocky's doing just fine.

Clancy is an Irish Setter who lives in South Jamesport, Long Island, New York, with Laurie Kauffman. He began barking early one morning, waking Ms. Kauffman. When she looked out the window, the street was dark and empty, the temperature below freezing. Clancy didn't stop barking. Ms. Kauffman opened the door, and there was a brown supermarket bag just alongside her doorstep. Inside the bag, to her amazement, was an infant, about two hours old, weighing 4 and ¾ pounds, a scant 18 inches long.

"The baby wasn't making any noise that I could hear,"

said Ms. Kauffman, who works as a substitute teacher. "If Clancy hadn't awakened me, I don't know how long it might have been before he was found."

Police were called, and they took the child to Central Suffolk Hospital in Riverhead. He had been born one to two hours before Ms. Kauffman had found him, and it was obvious that it had been an unattended birth. The umbilical had not been tied. The baby was reported in good condition.

As Ms. Kauffman later explained, "Clancy is a pretty good watchdog. He usually sleeps in my room, and this morning, when he was at that window, barking to wake me up, I knew that whatever he wanted was right outside. There was the baby, naked, in the bag. I took the child out and wrapped it in towels."

"Clancy," she went on, "is the famous dog that failed obedience school. He didn't exactly fail. I have his graduation certificate. But he wasn't the best, he was much too playful. Till today. Today he was all business!"

The police have thus far been unable to find the child's mother. But if Clancy could talk, he'd probably be able to give them a good description, for he *had* to have seen her!

Have you ever heard about Turkey? Turkey is a mongrel that was awarded the Certificate of Merit of the American Society for the Prevention of Cruelty to Animals.

During the great blizzard of February 1978, Michael Zezima was walking toward his Long Beach, New York, home when he happened upon a woman who was unable to make her way home through the snow. The snow had drifted waist high, and she just couldn't go any farther. Mike helped her to the home of one of her friends and then tried to continue on his way to his own home two blocks farther.

On the way, Mike collapsed from cold, snow, and wind.

A neighborhood stray that Mike had fed occasionally saw him lying in the snow. The dog lay down over Mike, covering him with his own body to keep him warm. He stayed with Mike for three hours this way, and finally, by barking, managed to attract the attention of passersby who sent for the fire department, which rescued Mr. Zezima.

At Long Beach Hospital, the dog refused to leave Mike, who was unconscious and suffering from exposure. Dr. Jane O'Shaughnessy, director of the emergency room, said, "I would credit the dog with saving the man's life." The animal was allowed to stay at the hospital and continued its vigil for the next ten hours.

When Mike Zezima recovered, he adopted the dog and named him Turkey. The ASPCA is proud to recognize Turkey as the embodiment of the concept of "Man's Best Friend."

Animals have a certain sense of danger that seems, very often, to elude man. How many times have you seen or heard absolutely nothing, yet your dog, who has been quietly lying at your feet, will suddenly become alert, sit up, and cock his head to one side, listening or sniffing tentatively.

Sam was a German shepherd living with a family in Long Island, New York. Sam was strictly a pet, and his usual household duties were limited to such things as lolling on the lawn and playing with the family's children. One of the children was an infant, and on a warm, sunny day the mother of the house placed the child in a playpen on the front lawn of their suburban home. Sam was told to "watch the baby," but this was almost a joke, for he simply did what he did best, i.e., sprawled on the lawn. The lady of the house laughed at Sam's obvious lack of concern. She went into the house, planning to keep an eye on the youngster from the kitchen window which looked out over the lawn.

Before long, Sam sensed trouble and became restive. He got up and came through the small pet-port door and into the kitchen, whimpering. He was obviously agitated, but there seemed no reason. Everything outside seemed calm and placid. The baby was asleep in the playpen. Under the woman's admonishments, Sam went back outside and sat on the lawn.

What happened next happened very quickly. An old lady with obvious mental problems lifted the baby from the playpen, placed him in a small perambulator, and continued her way up the street. Sam followed the lady at a safe distance, keeping a watchful eye on her. She made her way to a local shopping area, and it was at about that time that the baby was found to be missing. The police were called, and a search was made.

The poor mother was distraught. She called the neighbors in to help. Finally, a complete stranger, noticing the kidnapper's eccentric behavior, called a nearby police officer, who took her into custody. The child was returned to its parents, and Sam was also apprehended, for he seemed reluctant to part company with the child. The "arresting" officer checked Sam's collar, and the tag identified his name and address. The police officer called Sam's owners to inform them that Sam had been found, and the distraught mother exclaimed, "You found my dog? Good! Now how about my baby!" "Oh," the officer replied, "we found him, too!"

Actually, Sam had done precisely what he had been told to do—watch the baby.

To most people who have never been owned by a cat, the feline seems worthless except as a very independent pet that will, at the very most, tolerate its owners. But actually, cats are dependent, affectionate, and very devoted. Again, those who are not familiar with them seem to think that cats are stupid, for they will not come when called and do not learn "tricks" the way a dog does.

But cats are indeed devoted to their families, and cat owners will argue that, far from being stupid, they are just too smart to learn the dumb tricks that you can teach a dog. "After all," the cat might reason, "why should I roll over, just because you tell me to?"

One character in *Bell, Book and Candle*, a popular Broadway play of the 1950s, was a black cat named Pyewacket. Many household pets were subsequently given this strange, appealing name. Often it was shortened to Pie, and one mathematician redubbed it Pi!

One particular Pie lived with a family in Wilton, Connecticut, and made her livelihood as a pet. When the mood struck her, she'd loll on her back and allow her tummy to be scratched. When she'd had enough, she would nip lightly at the fingers, then haughtily get up, stretch, and move elsewhere. She had a good life, stretching to full length on the windowsill where she could soak up the morning sun and watch the tempting birds flitting through the trees.

At night, Pie was even more independent. She'd wait until everyone else was asleep, then hop to the foot of her master's bed. She would spend the night there, but jump down before morning. She did not want to admit that she liked sleeping near her master!

On the fateful night in question, a fire broke out in the attic of the home. Firemen later said that it was caused by spontaneous combustion of a pile of clothing thrown in a corner of the attic. The fire smoldered for a long while before the smoke began to seep down the stairwell and through the walls. When the smoke was sufficiently heavy, fire broke out. Pie knew that something was wrong almost at once. She awoke, sniffed the air, and then meowed loudly to try and wake her master. When he didn't respond, she climbed next to his face and called again. He pushed her aside in his sleep, and again she tried to awaken him. Finally, she hit his cheek with her paw, again and again.

At last he got up to see what the problem was. He walked into the hall and saw the thick smoke. He awakened the rest of the household and got them out, then called the fire department.

In piecing the story together later, he decided that if Pie had not been there, if she had not awakened him, the chances are that the entire family might never have awakened. The smoke would have overcome them as they slept, and then, unchecked, the fire would have destroyed their home, taking them with it.

Pyewacket was rewarded in terms that any cat would understand. She got a huge bowl of fresh liver, prepared just for her, and she gorged herself until her tummy was a hard round ball. After this delightful repast, she jumped to the windowsill, lay in the sun, and preened herself, purring happily all the time.

Percy is a Doberman pinscher who lives with the Greenberg family in New York City. Mrs. Greenberg was taking Percy for his regular daily walk in the park, keeping him on leash, as that is the law in New York. Her purse was loosely slung over her shoulder, and she carried a "pooper-scooper" (another New York City ordinance) in the other hand.

There were other people around, and Percy was behaving quite nicely when a young man approached Mrs. Greenberg, smiling pleasantly. He said, "Nice dog. Is he vicious?"

"Oh, of course not!" Mrs. Greenberg replied. "He's a little pussycat!"

With this, the dog snarled and growled. The youth backed off warily. "You sure he doesn't bite?" the boy asked.

"He never bites anybody!"

"Then give me your purse."

Nowadays, Mrs. Goldberg has a different tack. When asked if Percy is a biter, she assures all strangers that he is, and she tells them, "Please don't say the word k-i-l-l."

Dogs are extremely possessive and tend to guard their own territories very carefully. Let a stranger approach that territory, and you'll hear some loud and threatening barking. Some years ago, a long-haired shepherd named Wolfgang Amadeus Pooch lived with his family in New York City. The children took Wolf, as he was called, to the park for a romp. There, some tough youngsters made an attempt to relieve the children of their pocket money, bicycles, and valuables.

As the strangers came closer, the hackles on the back of Wolf's neck rose. He eyed them warily and moved closer to the family members. The toughs tried to brazen it out by surrounding the children. Now that they had crossed the line of Wolf's "turf," he became very agitated.

"Gimme that bike!" demanded one of them.

"And your money, too," said another.

"And hold that dog!" declared a third.

The kids were frightened. They tried to back away, but they were surrounded, and there was no place to go. Panicked, they looked around for an adult. The park suddenly seemed deserted.

The toughs were now closing in.

Wolf bared his fangs, curled his lip back, and snarled. They eyed him carefully and slowed in their advance.

"Wolf!" the young boy commanded, "Get 'em!"

Wolf barked, crouched, and leaped toward the tallest of the strangers, all of whom quickly took to their heels. The one Wolf was after got nipped on the leg. When he was called, Wolf returned to the kids' side.

The strangers in their flight saw a policeman and reported to him that some kids in the park had a real live wolf. They seemed genuinely frightened, so the cop came back with them to investigate. He asked the youngsters about the dog and they explained his name. The policeman smiled. They went on to explain their run-in with the strangers, and when the policeman turned to ask them about it, they simply ran away once again, thereby admitting their guilt. The patrolman released the youngsters, admonishing them to keep Wolf on his leash. He patted Wolf on the head and went on his way.

It was a warm summer day in Islip, New York, and the mother of the house put her baby in the backyard to play. There was no obvious element of danger apparent, as the entire yard was enclosed by a hurricane fence. The family's cocker spaniel, a pup named Flossie, was also released to the yard, and the lady of the house went on about her regular household chores, planning to keep an occasional eye on the child.

But danger did indeed rear its head in the form of a shallow plastic wading pool. This was a fixture in the backyard, and the woman never gave it a second thought. However, the youngster spotted the pool and made straight for it. Before long, the tyke had fallen into the pool, and the slippery sides made it impossible to climb out. In panic, the child fell face forward, unable to breathe, and was actually drowning in the shallow water in the pool.

That's when Flossie came to the rescue. She ran to the pool, grabbed the youngster's clothing in her sharp teeth, and pulled with all her might. Her strength was insufficient to pull the child out of the pool, but when the child's mother next looked out the window, she saw the dog struggling valiantly to pull the child out of the water. The child was crying and screaming, barely held above water by the dog. The woman rushed outside and snatched the child from the water.

Lady is a black Labrador retriever who lives on the coast of Maine with her master. It was their usual habit to go for a romp along the beach every morning, where he tossed driftwood into the waves for Lady to fetch. This was their regular morning game, and it was almost ritual.

One morning, they were taking their usual stroll when a cry was heard. Just beyond the breakers a young boy, alone in the water, was caught in the undertow. He couldn't make it back to shore.

Lady and her master heard the screams at the same time. While the master looked quickly for additional help—there was none—Lady plunged into the torrent and paddled to the young boy, who was trying to keep afloat. She reached him, and he caught hold of her coat with what may have been the last remains of his strength. He clung for dear life as Lady paddled back to shore.

As soon as they were free of the undertow and he could feel the solid bottom under his feet, he pulled himself the rest of the way to shore.

Lady? She took the entire rescue in a very matter-of-fact way. She sniffed at the boy, and when she realized that he was all right, she began romping and prancing again, trying to induce her master to toss another stick into the surf!

Old English sheepdogs are big balls of fur, white on one end and gray on the other. For the most part, these big, lovable teddy bears are rascals and clowns. They'll usually do anything for a laugh, and I recall teaching an obedience training class where the dogs were learning the command "Sit!" One Old English was having a problem. His young mistress was hollering at him and tugging at his leash. It looked as though the dog was sitting properly, and I asked why she was trying to correct him.

"This stupid dog has the wrong end down!" she shouted, still tugging at the leash.

Brucie is an Old English sheepdog who lives with his family in Fort Lauderdale, Florida, on a nice quiet street with little traffic. The youngster of the house was playing on the sidewalk one day, dragging a pull-toy after him. His mother came to the front door just in time to see what took place.

The child, about three years old, had wandered into the roadway, and a car was coming. The car was moving at high speed. Horrified, the child's mother knew she was too far away to keep the obvious accident from happening. Struck motionless by the impending tragedy, she clutched at her breast and gasped.

That's when Brucie moved into action. He jumped into the road, grabbed the child by the arm, and turned him back toward the sidewalk just in the nick of time.

Most Dalmatians that live in firehouses are considered working dogs, but for the most part they're really the firemen's pets. They have no "duties" except to ride on the fire trucks when the mood strikes them.

But Trixie is a Dalmatian who takes her work very seriously. When fire broke out in a home in Oklahoma City, Oklahoma, the local fire company rushed to the scene with Trixie sitting atop the big red engine. The fire, when the truck arrived, was a holocaust. The hoses were broken loose and played on the flames, and the valiant fire fighters did their best to contain and control the blaze.

Before anybody could stop her, Trixie ran into the blazing building and, despite the calls of the firemen, she wouldn't come out.

Finally they saw her emerge, crawling backward out

the front door. As soon as they could, the firemen rushed to her aid, to find that Trixie was dragging the family's pet, a cairn terrier, in her jaws. Both dogs received severe burns and had to be taken to the veterinarian for treatment.

Trixie is back at the firehouse now, and she boasts a nice medal on her collar, made by one of the firemen in his spare time.

Have you ever wondered how the barking of a dog—even the smallest dog—will make a would-be burglar think twice about breaking into a house? It's an interesting point in psychology.

A human being can be reasoned with—even a man with a gun. If a burglar breaks into a home and sees an armed homeowner with a pistol or a shotgun, he can yell, "Don't shoot!" and put his hands in the air. But you can't reason with a dog. If a burglar hears a dog barking, he's not going to enter that home, for a painful bite—or worse—may be the result.

A burglar in Boonton, New Jersey, learned this the hard way. He had "cased" his intended victim's home and knew that the family had a little fox terrier. He wasn't concerned about this, for he thought that all he had to do was say, "Nice doggie," and pat the pup on the head.

On the night of the robbery, he entered stealthily through an open window. The dog began barking. Then it grabbed hold of the man's leg and wouldn't let go. The dog's barking awakened the master of the house who that very week had obtained a pistol permit from his local police department. The man removed his gun from the dresser drawer in the bedroom and came down the stairs to see what the rumpus was.

Here was the burglar, dancing about the room, shaking his leg to get away from the dog, saying over and over again, "Nice doggie, nice doggie."

"Hold it!" the homeowner commanded. His wife called the police, and as they led the culprit from the house, he turned toward the dog and said, "Whatsa matter with you? Didn't I say 'nice doggie'?"

CHAPTER SIX

WORKING ANIMALS

Since the time man and beast first shared the earth, they have cooperated in performing tasks necessary to life. Man knew what had to be done, and the beast helped to do it. When a field needed plowing, man built the plow and guided the horse, who lent his tremendous strength to the task. Thanks to the shared effort, the grain was planted and harvested.

Animals have worked with man in numerous ways. Our good friends, the horses, have provided transportation. Dogs have worked as sled-pullers, as guide dogs furnishing eyes to the blind, and as guards. Animals have always shared man's common burden. The animal used for a particular task depends to a great extent on the location. In the sands of the arid, desert regions, camels are employed more than other beasts. In the South American countries, it is the llama that is the beast of burden. In Asia, one finds yaks and oxen put to use. The choice depends on the locale and on the docility of the animals involved.

Those of us who live in a given location are familiar with seeing animals of a specific sort used for a specific job. We raise our eyebrows, however, when we hear about other beasts being used for other work in other countries. For example, the cat is rarely thought of as a working animal, but in Siam cats are placed on small shelves over entry doors, where they stand guard over the house. Let an intruder try to enter, and the cat will drop onto his shoulders, clawing and scratching. In India and Burma, the mongoose is a working animal, protecting hut-dwellers from snakes of all sorts.

There have been many cases where work animals have rescued their masters from dangerous circumstances, thereby assuming more of the burden than they were originally meant to!

CERTIFICATE OF MERIT

For Distinguished Service

PRESENTED BY

The American Society for the Prevention of Cruelty to Animals

Pride
TO

On June 30, 1978, Pride, a 17 year old bay gelding and his rider, Police Officer Eugene Kempton, were stationed at their usual post near Nassau and Fulton Streets in the Wall Street area of Manhattan when an ice cream truck exploded with tremendous force ten feet away from them. Police Officer Kempton was thrown from the saddle while Pride was literally hurled into the air. Over 150 people were injured from the explosion. Although hurt himself, Police Officer Kempton called for police, fire and ambulance service and gave first aid to others who were injured. In the meantime, Pride, as noted in newspaper accounts, "acted in the finest tradition, remaining calm and staying by his rider, even though hit by flying glass and bits of metal, and in obvious pain." Pride's hind legs and right foreleg were cut with glass and metal. These painful injuries did not send Pride running wild in a panic-stricken street. His steadfast behavior was that of a seasoned veteran. For this outstanding feat, which demonstrated his great courage and utilization of his proficient training, the ASPCA proudly presents Pride with its Medal of Honor and Certificate of Merit.

_____
President

Horses are often skittish. Any rider can tell stories about how he was riding peacefully when a stray leaf or piece of paper caught the wind and flitted up toward the horse. The horse balks, rears, and the rider is thrown to the ground. Any sudden noise will have the same effect. Startle a horse—and it seems that almost anything will startle him—and you're sitting on your duff.

Pride was a police mount—a seventeen-year-old bay gelding—stationed in the heart of New York City's financial district. This is a very overcrowded area. Cars, trucks, taxicabs, and people compete for whatever space is available. The streets are narrow, it's noisy, and people spill off the sidewalks into the streets. It's a constant hubbub and more than enough to frighten people, let alone horses!

Police Officer Eugene Kempton was on duty with Pride on June 30, 1978, when an ice cream truck exploded not ten feet away from them. Officer Kempton was thrown from the saddle. Pride was literally hurled into the air. Over 150 people were injured as a result of the blast.

Kempton was hurt, but he managed to call for the necessary emergency services that gave aid to the injured. The scene was a confusing melee of fire trucks, policemen, and ambulances. In all this confusion, Pride remained calm. He remained true to the police tradition and stayed by Kempton's side, though injured by flying glass and bits of metal and obviously in great pain. His right foreleg and both hind legs were badly cut, but his steadfast behavior was that of a seasoned veteran.

For this outstanding feat, which demonstrated his great courage and the utilization of his proficient training, Pride was awarded the Medal of Honor of the ASPCA and a certificate of merit.

Star is a Seeing Eye dog who lived with the Logue family of Brooklyn, New York. Ellen Logue, who is blind, was alone in their house when fire broke out. The Logues' sons, Richard, twenty-five, and Michael, twenty-three, who are also blind as a result of a heriditary condition, and William, nineteen, who is partially blind, were not at home.

A fourth son, Peter, who has normal vision, was away at school.

After leading Ellen Logue to safety, Star tried to return to the conflagration to save the lives of two cats that were trapped by the flames in one of the boys' rooms. However, there was just too much flame, and Star couldn't get to the cats in time to save them.

The Logues are aware that Star is a hero, for while she was trained as a guide dog, the saving of Ellen Logue's life was a service above and beyond the call of duty.

The New York City Police Department recently took a rather unusual step in awarding an official certificate of appreciation to Fang, a stray mongrel. This probably marks the first time that such a citation has been offered. "A dog? A d-o-g?" One police official scratched his head and wondered. Detective Alfred Young, the Police Department's historian, said, "I don't have any record of any other dog outside the Department receiving such an award." Citations usually went to bomb-squad dogs who sniff out explosives, or, more recently, dogs used to detect contraband or drugs. But a civilian dog? Never.

Fang was a stray, living out of garbage cans, who was adopted by the Pelham Parkway Block Association. Fang, who is lean and mostly black and tan, seems to be a mixture of collie, German Shepherd, and who-knows-what, became an unofficial member of the Block Association after having been hit by a car on the Bronx River Parkway.

Roy Israel, attorney for the Association, stopped to rescue Fang and had his car demolished for his efforts. "We called him the $4,200 dog because of Roy's car," explained Leonard Gordon, president of the Association. "Another car plowed into Roy's on the shoulder, while he was trying to get Fang off the road."

With so much trouble already invested in their dog, they decided to go all the way and bring Fang to a veterinarian. Fang's teeth were broken, and that's how he got his name. He was so bruised that he could not walk, but he managed to recover and became the association's watchdog.

Fang proved his worth when burglars broke through a window of the Association's basement suite. The police rousted Gordon out of bed at 5 A.M. to inform him of the attempted break-in. Gordon came to quiet Fang, who would not even allow the police to come in and investigate.

There must have been quite a row, for chairs were overturned, and other items were strewn about. The burglars left without a thing.

At the award ceremony, Capt. James Trainor commented, "This dog has repaid his debt to the people who took him in and gave him a home."

The two hundred or so spectators broke into a vigorous round of applause, and Fang responded with a smart wagging of his tail, one of the most endearing of acceptance speeches ever.

"He's the most popular dog on Pelham Parkway," Gordon says. "Maybe we ought to run him for office next year!"

Not all animal hero stories end on such a positive note. A dog hero—at least one who tried to be—has been adopted by the police whom she helped summon. She tried vainly to save her masters in a fire in Jamaica, New York. The fire, which killed Mr. and Mrs. Arthur McCormack, both sixty-eight, was discovered when the dog awakened a neighbor by scratching and whimpering at their door.

The now homeless dog, mostly German shepherd, was taken to the 107th Precinct in Fresh Meadows, but when the stationmaster said there was no room for a mascot, she was turned over to Highway Unit Three, in Queens. The dog, of course, had no name. She was called Julia, after Captain Julius Moskowitz, and then Smokey, referring to her act of heroism.

Now the dog has settled in with her new friends. She takes potluck with the policemen. They bring in scraps and other offerings, but it seems that she's partial to bagels with butter in the morning!

Lewis is a Doberman pinscher who is called, affectionately, Louie. Louie is the constant friend and companion of Ronald McNee, who owns and operates a service station. Louie was given his name because the first person he ever bit was named Robert Lewis. Ronnie settled on that name to placate the offended "bitee."

Generally, Ron works alone, and one night he was unable to fall asleep. He whistled Louie up, got into his truck, and headed for the service station, thinking that there might be some mechanical work he could do on one of his cars, rather than just tossing and turning in bed all night.

It was about 2 A.M. The gas station was officially closed and the pump lights were out. Ron had a car on the lift and was working under it. He saw a pair of headlights turn into the station and stop at the pumps. He went to the door and called, "We're closed—sorry!"

One of the men got out of the car and approached the door. Ron could see several others inside the car. "Can you open the door and give me some directions?" the man asked.

Ron replied, "I can hear you all right. Where do you want to go?"

At this point, Louie entered the picture, and sat next to Ron in plain view.

"I'm not afraid of your dog," the man said, and two others from the car joined him. One had a tire iron in his hand. "Now open the door," he said.

Ron eyed the men carefully. He moved back, away from the door, and went to the phone to call the police. One of the men said, "If you don't open the door, we'll smash the glass. Now move!"

Ron knew what would happen. He complied and opened the door. Louie waited for no further invitation. He was all over the men in a trice, snapping, growling and baring his fangs.

"Call 'im off!" one of the men shouted as they retreated to their car.

They left hurriedly but not until Ron had gotten the

license-plate number. He jotted it down, noted the year and make of the car and the direction in which it was headed. He notified the local police, who alerted several radio cars. The men were apprehended and brought back the next day for Ron's identification. Louie was still there. He sniffed at the men's clothing and started to growl. "Well, Ron," one of the policemen said, "it seems that Louie knows these guys!"

Have you ever heard a story about an attack-trained rabbit?

Harvey had originally been purchased as an Easter bunny, but was mistreated—probably with sticks, pencils, and too-loving bear hugs—but had to learn to defend himself. As his skill and proficiency in defense grew, he was left more and more on his own. Finally his family turned him in to the ASPCA for biting. How many people had he bitten? Six in all, up to that point.

The director of the ASPCA put his hand into the cage to pet Harvey. Harvey bit him. Another worker tried the same thing, and got the same result.

Harvey had to work for his keep. At night, he was given free run of the office, where he served as a guard. Any individual who tried to break in would have been beset by a furious, angry, snapping bunny.

There was no way to tell how Harvey would react to people. He bit a couple of female Playboy Club employees, which just shows that this little rabbit had little taste for bunnies.

Harvey became a hero and eventually a celebrity. He has appeared on television and has brought the Society a great deal of publicity for their campaigns against animal cruelty.

Harvey T-shirts were (and still are) very popular. In addition to a picture of Harvey, they state "This property protected by Harvey, the Attack Rabbit."

Then one day Harvey developed an ear infection. Now to a rabbit, I suppose an ear infection can be as serious as a throat infection can be to a giraffe. This one proved too much, and Harvey succumbed just before Easter.

133

"Cantankerous old rabbit," somebody said. "I'll just bet he died before Easter on purpose!"

Before his death, Harvey had become something of a ham. One of his tricks consisted of tossing his food bowl high in the air. When it landed, he'd try to get all four-and-one-half pounds of Harvey into the four-inch bowl. If the bowl landed upside down, this presented a problem.

He was also learning—or trying to learn—how to center a ball, but his hind legs kept getting in the way.

Harvey's gone now, to a hero's reward. Gone, but not forgotten.

A guard dog cannot be called a hero simply for doing the work it is trained to do. However, let the dog do something above and beyond the call of duty and that is a different matter. That's the way Patrolman Fred Fleecer, of the Banford, New Jersey, Police Department feels about his partner Flicker, a German shepherd guard dog.

One evening, they were walking their beat when they happened on a holdup in progress. The action was taking place in a liquor store, and the man behind the counter was standing with his arms upraised. Another man faced him, his back to the door, a pistol in his hand. Patrolman Fleecer drew his service revolver and quietly entered the store. "Put the gun down," he said quietly. The youth whirled about and fired a shot at Fleecer. The storekeeper dropped to the floor behind the counter. The shot was fired at close range and nicked Fred's shoulder, causing him to drop his own gun. At this point, Flicker leaped into action. He went for the criminal's gun hand, locking his massive jaws around the wrist. The man screamed and tried to shake Flicker loose. He managed to transfer the gun to his other hand and beat Flicker about his head with the butt. Under the punishing blows, Flicker loosened his grip and fell to the floor.

The man pocketed his gun, swore at the fallen officer, and fled from the store. Flicker picked himself up, shook his bleeding head, and threw a glance at his partner, Fred. Seeing that Fred was slowly getting to his feet, the dog turned his attention to the fleeing criminal and raced out of the store after him.

Seeing the dog coming after him, the holdup man turned and pegged off one shot from the street. Passersby ducked for cover. Wounded in his right thigh, the dog continued single-mindedly. Fleecer was radioing for assistance, and police cars began to arrive, effectively blocking the street. The dog got to the fleeing gunman before the men did. When they apprehended him, Flicker's jaws were clamped to the man's wrist. The dog continued to hold the man's gun hand as the police came up, guns drawn. A police-trained dog will normally await his partner for a call-off, but if his partner is not available, he will respond to a command from any policeman. This Flicker did, releasing the gunman. Then he fell to the pavement, unconscious from loss of blood.

The man's arm had been severely lacerated. He was taken under guard to the ambulance and then to the hospital. He is, at the time of this writing, serving a sentence in the state prison.

As the store owner explained later, the crime itself had not been planned. It just seemed to happen. The youth ambled into the store to make a purchase. When he was told the price, he found that he was short of funds and offered to pay what he had. The storekeeper refused this and reached for the merchandise. The youth pulled out the pistol, explaining that if he couldn't buy the stuff, he'd just steal it. Then, as an afterthought, he said, "As long as I'm stealing anyway, empty the cash register, too."

That's when Fleecer, walked in and the shooting started.

Flicker was rushed to the nearest veterinarian by the police. His thigh wound was superficial and healed nicely. His head wounds must have left him with an awful headache for a while, but he is back on duty with Fleecer whose own wounds have also healed.

Jim Winters runs a sheep farm in Montana, and his daily chores include taking the flock up the slope of a nearby mountain where they spend the day grazing. As company, he takes along Kim, a large collie who helps keep the sheep in close position. Kim has also learned a few tricks which most collies do not ordinarily master. Kim has learned that when there's a good ball game on the air, she's supposed to sleep at Jim's feet with one eye open on the flock, while he props himself under a convenient tree and listens to the game on his transistor radio. And if there isn't a game on, Jim sometimes goes off in search of some suitable game that might grace the dinner table that night. Kim has learned to flush game for Jim and can even take a point.

Jim rarely went after anything big, usually just birds or rabbits. He carried a .22 rifle with him, just in case, along with a pocketful of ball and bird shot cartridges, depending on what Kim might turn up.

One chilly day in early spring, Jim put on his big mackinaw, shouldered his .22, and put a handful of assorted shells in his pocket. He whistled Kim up, and they got the sheep out of the pen and moving toward the slope.

After the sheep were settled, Jim called to Kim and suggested they go look for some supper. He and the dog ambled off toward the wood. Suddenly, Kim froze and pointed. On the hunch that it might be a rabbit, Jim put a ball cartridge into the breech of the rifle. On his hissed signal, Kim dove barking into the grass, and with a fluttering of wings, sounding as loud as a motorboat, a covey of quail took to the air. 'Damn!" Jim shouted, shouldering the rifle and getting his single shot off. If he'd loaded with bird shot, he'd have had one for sure, but the ball simply flew into space, missing cleanly. The birds were long gone by the time he could reload.

Kim raised her snout and tasted the air. She sensed that something was amiss and nudged at Jim's leg, trying to herd him back to the flock. He had been in this game too long to mistrust his dog, and he turned back toward the sheep. When Kim saw that he was on the way, she rushed ahead.

When Jim arrived back at the flock, a bloody sight greeted him. Kim was trying to fight off a pack of coyotes, ravenous after long winter months on meager pickings. As a small part of the group attacked the flock at one side, another part of the coyote pack would attack at the other side, making it impossible for Kim to defend the sheep.

Jim fished in his pocket for the ball cartridges and loaded and fired as fast as he could. It wasn't long, however, before he ran out of cartridges. He waded into the fray, using the gunstock as a club.

The coyotes attacked him in a group. Jim did his best to fend them off, but they pressed the attack. His arms and legs were bleeding from multiple lacerations, and his arms were aching from swinging the rifle. Through this entire melee, Kim was by her master's side, trying to ward off the fangs of the attacking coyotes. She, too, had already suffered numerous bites about the legs and face.

Finally, the tide of battle turned, and the coyotes, seeing that this was not to be their day, turned and fled, leaving their dead and wounded fellows to their fates.

Kim approached her master, who was trying to take stock of both his own condition and the condition of his flock. Neither was in great shape. He sat down hard and looked at his dog. His head shook slowly and, weakened from loss of blood, he slipped senseless to the ground.

Up to this point, Kim had done her level best and more. Even now she did not give up. Despite her own wounds, despite her tiredness and failing strength, she went back down the hill to get help. She did not do this at once, for she feared that the coyotes might return. If a dog could ever be said to have reasoned like a person, Kim did so now. There was a possibility that the enemy might come back, but a certainty that Jim needed help. Kim headed back to the ranch as fast as she could go.

One look at her and the ranch hands knew something was amiss. One of the men grabbed his snap-on pistol holster. A group of the men followed Kim back up the hill to where Jim lay. They administered immediate first aid, then carried him to safety. At the hospital, his wounds were cleaned and bound up and he underwent the first of a long and painful series of shots for rabies. Kim had to be carried down the slope as well, for she was badly weakened. One of the men remained behind with the sheep, actually hoping that the coyotes might return so he could get even. They did not. To avoid the possibility of baiting the coyotes, the dead sheep were buried.

Kim recovered quickly. She received no special reward for her extra effort, except for a very affectionate pat on the head. Jim has changed his ways now. When he and Kim go up the slope with the sheep, Jim takes a varmint rifle along, with plenty of ammunition, and he lets somebody else worry about what's going to be on the dinner table!

It's not often that a man and an animal get the chance to perform heroically together, but this happened once about twenty-five years ago in Prospect Park in Brooklyn.

The park is a weekend refuge for city people, offering all sorts of diversions, including ball fields, band shells, roller-skating rinks, lakes for boating, and just quiet places covered with grass on which the people can sit and enjoy the summer breezes. The park also offers a fine bridle path and nearby stables from which horses can be rented. Often, people with no experience as equestrians will rent a horse and "just give it a try." As long as they have the required fee, they are given a horse and turned loose.

Unfortunately, they are often victimized by vicious young pranksters who amuse themselves by standing on one of the many stone bridges that span the bridle path, and, armed with small stones, wait for a rider to come through. When one does, they hurl the stones at the horse's rump, causing the horse to break into a gallop.

One young girl, out riding for the first time, fell victim to these kids. Her horse, after having been struck by a stone, broke into a full gallop, and the girl panicked. She fell forward over the horse's mane, dropping the reins and clutching at his neck, screaming and bouncing as she went.

A young man who had been trotting along behind the girl saw the entire thing, and when he realized that she had lost control, he kicked his own horse into a gallop and raced under the bridge after her.

In short order, he caught up with her and guided his own mount alongside the frightened, racing horse. "Over here!" he shouted. She turned toward him, frightened out of her wits. He put his arm around her waist and lifted her bodily from her saddle. She had already lost the stirrups. His plan was to hold her in this fashion while reining in his own horse, and when his horse had come to a complete halt, to lower her to the ground. He knew that her horse would follow the bridle path and return sooner or later to the stables. It was at this point that he noticed something. As his own horse slowed under the pressure of the reins, the girl's horse slowed also, and they stopped at the same time!

He looked down as he released the girl, and saw that his horse had taken the reins of the runaway in his teeth and had actually halted it! Back at the stable, the stable owner tried to talk the girl into going out again. As he said, "Once you fall off a horse, you just gotta get back on again, or you'll never ride no more!"

She took her money back instead and informed him that from now on she'd restrict her physical activities to dancing.

In a lighter vein, the mounted police troop of a large city was moving slowly along a busy avenue one day. They were strung out for about the length of a city block, moving in columns of ones and twos, when they passed a drunk on the sidewalk. The drunk moved to the curb for a better look. Then he started waving his hat and shouting, "C'mon Number 1173, c'mon Number 1173!"

Metropolitan troops are used primarily for traffic control and—when the occasion warrants—riot control. On one such occasion, the horse patrol was moving around the perimeter of a large, unruly mob, controlling and containing it as best they could. One rioter tried to pull a policeman from his horse. The horse turned to face the man, but too late. The policeman was on the ground, attacked from all sides by the rioters. Naturally, other officers rode to his rescue, their batons in action as they moved. But before they could clear a path to the downed patrolman, his mount swung into action.

The horse reared, and with front hooves flailing he quickly cleared the area around his partner. He stood his ground over the fallen officer, and as the crowd tried again and again to press in on the policeman, the horse would rear, his hooves moving rapidly. The crowd kept falling back, and before long, other policemen arrived close enough to take over the work of the heroic horse. Several arrests were made, the culprits were led away, and the rest of the crowd fell back to a safe distance while the injured officer was removed.

Like almost every other industry, the cattle industry has become automated. The cowboy has in many cases given up his four-legged mount in favor of a jeep, or in some cases even an airplane or a helicopter. Still, the romance of the Old West remains, and even though a bit less practical, the horse still gets more miles per pound of fodder than an internal combustion engine does to a gallon of gasoline!

One typical western cowpuncher was riding his horse back from the rangelands one afternoon when he dismounted at a stream for a cold drink of water. His horse, too, was thirsty. The man lay face down to slake his thirst and the horse took a position downstream for his own drink.

Suddenly the horse rose, his nostrils dilated, his eyes wild. He began rearing and coming down stiff-legged on his front hooves, whinnying all the time. Again and again, he came up and then dropped again, front legs stiffly before him. The cowboy wondered for a moment what was happening to his otherwise stolid mount. Then he looked down and saw the writhing rattlesnake, poising to strike, just in time to again be struck by the horse's hooves. The animal's timing was excellent, and the snake was getting far the worst of the battle, when the horse turned and took a few running steps away to come in again for the kill. By this time, the cowboy had removed the big .44 magnum from its holster, and with a few quick shots dispatched the snake.

The horse snorted, walked over to the man, and nudged him with his muzzle, as though to say, "Thank you" and "We did it."

CHAPTER SEVEN

THE OTHER SIDE OF THE COIN

Does man extend himself to defend the members of the animal kingdom? Of course he does! There are game and bird preserves and sanctuaries all over the world. Certain beasts and birds are listed as endangered species. We not only share the earth with animals, we want to go right on sharing it for a good long time.

Is this really important? I believe it is, for we already miss certain animals that once were commonplace and are now extinct. We can see these missing beasts and birds only through pictures, and this is a sad commentary.

But for every man who has set out to decimate the animal kingdom, others have taken a positive view and have striven to protect otherwise endangered beasts.

Perhaps a few case histories are in order at this point.

Consider the plight of a species of fish, smaller than a finger, that exists only in one river in the southern United States—a river that was eyed by one of the country's biggest electric power authorities as the prospective site of a huge generating plant. Ecologists pointed out that the fish would most certainly be exterminated—eliminated totally from the face of the earth—should this project be completed.

Those fish are still swimming in that river, and the huge hydroelectric plant proposed by the Tennessee Valley Authority is conspicuous by its absence. The government bowed to the wishes of the ecologists and halted the project so that the fish might live.

Harp seals are the subjects of a less encouraging story. Baby harp seals are hunted in an annual slaughter that brings men with bats and clubs to the whelping areas. The young are completely helpless. Because they are hunted for their pelts, clubbing is the only way to destroy them so that no disfiguring holes are made in the pelts. The seal herds were being decimated year by year, until a group of concerned people took matters into their own hands. They joined the hunters on the ice and literally threw their bodies across the bodies of the seals to prevent their murder. Although the action of these brave opponents to the slaughter helped to a degree, the killers still wreaked havoc nonetheless.

What *did* happen was that a great deal of public attention was focused on the mass murder of these hapless and helpless infants. While the law continues to sanction the annual kill, it appears that public sentiment is growing against the killers and that it may not be long before the baby harps are protected against this annual slaughter.

Whales are hunted from huge factory ships that operate in the North Atlantic. These ships have completely automated the destruction of the whales. Forget all you've read about the romance of the New England whalers, where the whale was hunted with a spear. Today, things are different. Modern technology doesn't give the whale a ghost of a chance.

The decimation of these huge beasts is such that the whale is now in danger of vanishing from the face of the earth. While it is true that man is the cause of this destruction, man is also making an effort to stop it.

People have taken to small boats during the whaling season to do all that is humanly possible to stem the invasion of the whaling waters. They sail their little ships between the hunter and the hunted, hold up placards begging the hunters to stop, and do anything and everything to save the whales from destruction. Again, as in the case of the baby harp seals, they are little more than a nuisance to the hunters. But they focus the public eye on what is happening, and each year pressure builds against the threat to the whales.

It must be pointed out that the saving of a rare or nearly extinct animal or bird in a zoological garden does not in the least count in the preservation of nature's plan. We must preserve the beasts of nature in the wild state.

To too many people, the safety of animals is an impersonal thing at best. Their "I can't do anything about it" attitude makes them as guilty in the final analysis as the people who are actually wielding the instruments of death and destruction.

If you aren't a part of the solution, then you're a part—a big part—of the problem.

ACKNOWLEDGMENTS

Thanks are due to Kathy Rand of the Ken-L-Ration Division of the Quaker Oats Company. She helped to a fantastic extent, with stories, photos, and encouraging words, all the way from Chicago.

Tom Cathro is another important friend, for he is deeply steeped in circus lore. As a long time circus employee, he filled me in on many yarns about life on the back lot. And thanks to Tom, I now know the difference between a "donnaker" and a "clem." Tom is now one of the country's top performing magicians. See Tom? I *did* get in a plug for you!

There's a difference between loving animals and *knowing* about animals. I've always loved 'em, but Susie Wofsey, of Happicairn Kennels, taught me much about what I now know. Thanks Susie, and kiss all the "kids" for me.

Support also came from numerous quarters; Cindy Renner, Cathy Hughes, Sydell, Fern and Lori Rubin, My Dad, Joe Wels, who tolerantly accepted the strays I brought home as a youngster, and my own kids, Josh, Debbie and Heather, who did the same, trying my own patience in their turn.